THESE PEOPLE KNOW TOM FELTENSTEIN

Read what these people have to say about the man and his book:

UNCOMMON WISDOM
Live a Joyful Life
With Financial Success

"Tom Feltenstein is a remarkable man with an unusual ability to stand outside the ordinary paradigm and offer his readers a new way of seeing. In *Uncommon Wisdom,* Tom presents an uncommonly rich mix of mind-opening quotations and penetrating insights. Drawing from the teachings of many traditions, he reveals the secrets of the art of living."
—*Dinabandhu, Executive Director*
Omega Institute for Holistic Studies

"Tom Feltenstein's writings reach out like a large hand and grab us off the treadmill of life. He turns us sideways and pokes the light into our darkest corners of everyday activities so that we stop and look and see *why.* His insights are revolutionary. His depth of understanding triggers our need to know more. It will help you get rid of the clutter in your life as well as the clutter in your mind. Don't miss the opportunity to read this great book."
—*Bernard Hale Zick,*
author, Advice for the Impatient Investor

"What a delight! What a treasure trove of ideas and practices! Your book will add immeasurably to the aliveness of many people. It is a sourcebook of truly 'uncommon wisdom.' I know I will draw heavily on it in my own personal and professional journey."
—*Richard Barnes,*
Unity Center of New York

"I feel Mr. Feltenstein's book is an important step in returning healthy ethics to the business community. Money is not God, but the financial world surely projects that message. His suggestion is that life's true wealth is measured in things far more soulful than property, and we had better put them into our life, as a way of life, if the human business community is ever to recapture its humanity."
—*Patch Adams, M.D.*

"I am presently in the middle of five other books but had little trouble putting them away and finishing yours this past weekend.

"What a heartfelt experience it was to slow down and reflect on what gives your life meaning and joy in and out of the business world. It is very close to the vision I hold, and it affirmed that the business arena is just another opportunity to touch people's lives and be touched in a deep and lasting way.

"I especially enjoyed your thoughts on integrity, enlightenment, and the Seven Laws of Success. It is difficult to live a life with such a courageous vision, but I can see that there is no other choice for you."
—*Peter Sarris,*
president, T-Bones Great American Eatery

"*Uncommon Wisdom* is a fun, refreshing, and imaginative look at common sense and entertaining stress-reduction techniques. Extremely readable and thought-provoking, if not inspiring."
—*Bill Main,*
International Business Consultant

"Tom Feltenstein did it again! *Uncommon Wisdom* is a celebration of life. It is a refreshing and upbeat compilation of time-proven 'pearls of wisdom,' practical insights, and spiritual guidance that inspires success in what it means to be human. Tom's style is clear, direct, easy to read, and riddled with humor. Taken as a whole, *Uncommon Wisdom* manages to weave together, in a joyful and entertaining manner, the millennial teachings of humankind and our most progressive views on self, relations, change, business, and healing, and it suggests a lifestyle founded upon love, truth, and serendipity. In essence, it is a highly practical manual for living comfortably in an all-too-uncomfortable world. Read it and you'll *be* it!"
—*Oscar Miro-Quesada, M.A., Psy.Et., psychotherapist, international lecturer, and consultant, author and creator of* PSI*KICK: The Game

"... an uncommonly good book, a guide for both men and women preoccupied with today's ever-increasing busy busyness, the feeling of being caught on a treadmill with no way out and, just as important, no ability to change the pace of that treadmill. Dear Tom, I congratulate you on an enticing book, one that teaches us to let go of past dreams and move on to the future. It's excellent!"
—*Deborah Szekely,*
founder, Golden Door

"My prediction: Literary critics and book reviewers will enthusiastically commend, hail, and applaud your latest writing, so that *Uncommon Wisdom* will accelerate to the top-ten list of books."
—*Frank Wright,*
president, Palm Beach Round Table

"Until now, I always believed that there were some ideas that just couldn't be put into words. Tom Feltenstein has changed my mind. He has found a way to reveal little-known secrets about the human condition in such an interesting and provocative manner. Tom takes the wisdom of the ages and uses it to gently coax the reader to heal the places in the mind where psychological problems originate. This book is not an empty promise. It's the key to self-transformation."
—*Bill Gove,*
past president, National Speakers Association,
recipient, "Golden Gavel" Award

"Another winner, Tom! You were born to share your very human experiences through literature!

"I treasure every paragraph. My frustration is wanting to re-read the last while bursting to drink in the next! You are helping me—and my family—to discover the 'awakened life.' "
—*Ty Boyd,*
Ty Boyd Enterprises, Inc.

"You're all right, Tom. God has given you a great mind and many talents. The challenge is to give them the glory, and I think you are doing that in so many ways in your writings."
—*Mary Smith,*
president, Wojtusik, Smith & Associates

■ About the Author

Tom Feltenstein has redefined the word *humanist* for the millennium—enriching the term with a sense of self that transcends the traditional roles of father, husband, author, entrepreneur, lecturer, marketing and franchising executive, athlete, CEO, philanthropist, and community leader. Tom has published more than half a dozen books and, as chairman of Tom Feltenstein's Neighborhood Marketing Institute, is recognized as one of the country's leading authorities on strategic marketing.

Tom complements his frequent lectures, seminars, and workshops with media appearances on such programs as the *David Letterman Show* and Financial News Network's *Midday Market Report.*

Through insight, stories, cartoons, and a profound sharing of over two decades of correspondence with people all over the world, Tom eloquently touches on the most important issues in all of our lives.

Uncommon Wisdom

Other Books by Tom Feltenstein

—

Life—Making It Work for You

Life From A to Z

Foodservice Marketing for the '90s

Tom Feltenstein's Encyclopedia of 333 Promotional Tactics

Restaurant Profits Through Advertising & Promotion

Underdog Marketing

Uncommon Wisdom

*Live a Joyful Life
With Financial Success*

Tom Feltenstein

Lebhar-Friedman Books is a company of Lebhar-Friedman Inc.

Printed in the United States of America

Library of Congress Cataloging-in-Publication Data

Feltenstein, Tom.
    Uncommon wisdom : live a joyful life with financial success / Tom Feltenstein.
        p. cm.
    Includes index.
    ISBN 0-86730-757-9 (hc. : alk. paper)
    1. Success—psychological aspects. 2. Success in business. I. Title.
II. Title: Live a joyful life with financial success. BF637, S8F42 1999
158.1—dc21   98-55760
                                                                       CIP

Visit our Internet site at www.lfbooks.com.

Volume Discounts

This book makes a great gift and incentive. Call (212) 756-5240 for
information on volume discounts.

Table of Contents

—

▬ Chapter Three

■ Chapter Four

■ Chapter Five

■ Chapter Six

■ Chapter Seven

■ Chapter Eight

■ Chapter Nine

■ Acknowledgments

Billy DeVoress, William Samuel, Yogi Amrit Desai, Oscar Miro-Quesada, my
sister Suzy Wiberg, and Mom—all inspiring teachers in spirit who showed
me practical ways to open my heart and love all beings.

My two beautiful children—Andrew and Jennifer. I love you. Thanks
for sharing your lives with me. I'm grateful for the "on the job training" in
parenting that you've afforded me. Talk about growing by leaps and
bounds daily! My deepest thanks to *all* my past teachers and other
sources of inspiration—too numerous to name—who are now a part of me.

■ Dedication

*To Kathy, and to my beautiful children, Andrew
and Jennifer, whom I love dearly.*

This book has been evolving over many years.
As I was pondering the preparation of this new book in the summer of 1991,
I began the journey with a request. A few months later, on December 17,
1991, my request was answered. I met my soulmate. Three weeks later, on
January 6, 1992, we were married.

Be careful what you ask for—it just may come true. Our lives are like a
journey up a mountain path. As we climb, we face challenges in relationships,
money, work, health, and sexuality. We can find abundant information and
advice about all of these subjects. Many of us know what to do, but to make
real changes in our lives, we have to turn knowing into doing. And that's what
I did. My beautiful wife, Kathy, has been my most profound mirror. She has
been there to assist me in turning my intentions into action, and my challenges
into strengths—what a blessing. I dedicate this book to Kathy. Her support,
encouragement, feedback, feistiness, and love have contributed to an accelera-
tion of my growth over the past seven years. Our partnership expands and
deepens daily. Thank you, Mrs. Feltenstein. I love you.

■ Preface

A Special Friend

There's a man I know who makes me think deep thoughts about myself. There's something special about this man. He takes each day in a simple way. It's as if he has learned secrets that very few know and holds the key to some wisdom he's found.

It's not money or power or position he holds ... he just celebrates being alive.

Sometimes he feels guilty, I think, for the way he lives—for his contentment just to be and to feel.

Yet he must know it's the world that he owns, and all that he has is for free.

It's not really a secret he's found. It's something each of us possesses.

It gets lost or just covered up sometimes—or we think that someone has taken it away.

So I'll hold on to the thoughts that he's made me think, and I'll be unafraid to grow.

For that's step one—the first thing to learn—if I want to be all I can be.

I'll never know all the thoughts of this man, this friend who touched my life way back in 1970.

But he touched my hand, and now I too know the truths he's found.

Thanks, Bill Samuel

■ Introduction

A Surgeon General's warning about this book would read: "Caution! This book is highly threatening to your current way of life. Further study of these pages might cause you permanent joy and tranquillity."

I was beginning to believe that distress, boredom, guilt, and indecisiveness were in some way divine retribution for how badly I had been behaving over the years. I thought I was happy, successful, and, oh, yes, enlightened about the ways of life, and I always thought that enlightenment and happiness were to be found over there—just around the corner. Now I realize that, in a sense, I had been asleep all of those years and dreaming I was awake. I had been looking for my happiness in new landscapes and new horizons, instead of just opening my eyes and finding them within. I was like a competitor in a javelin-throwing match who had won the toss and elected to receive.

With the help of some old and some new friends, I found that there are a number of available tools to assist in supporting my growth and well-being—tools I've been too macho to use in the past. I've learned a new word—*acceptance*—and I've learned to accept myself as I am. Whatever is happening in my life, I've chosen to accept. So now I can relax and enjoy the ride. I can have some fun and quit being so serious.

About a year ago, I read a book that touched my life significantly. I reviewed it again recently and listened to some of the author's cassette tapes. I want to share some thoughts, feelings, and insights from the writings of a new friend, Dan Millman.

In a recent interview Dan Millman, author of *Way of the Peaceful Warrior*, told *Vision* magazine a story about a wise man who was found searching for something under a street light across the road from his house. A friend asked what he was looking for, and the man said, "The keys to my door."

His friend asked, "Where did you drop them?" The man said, "I think somewhere near my door."

"Then why are you searching here, across the street?" the friend asked.

And the wise man answered, "Well, can't you see the light is much better here?"

I've been searching for acceptance and success out there under the street lamp, looking at what other people thought about my image. I was trying to look good on the outside while I felt unfulfilled on the inside. The battleground is inside. Dan Millman says, "We are all in the ring sparring with dark forces such as fear, apathy, insecurity, and self-doubt." These are demons combatted by angels of courage, commitment, and confidence. Our world is simply a reflection of how the battle is going. This has been hard for me to see, particularly when life has seemed to be good. Only when times seem bleak and dark did I begin to look at what is!

In the closing of *Peaceful Warrior,* Millman writes, "When you're comfortable the light will disturb you, and when you're disturbed the light will comfort you."

I want this book to talk to the real you. Not to the business or professional person you are, not to the family person, not even to the hobbyist—though they are all part of you. I wish to speak to that invisible, weightless part of you that will float away when it no longer inhabits your body. Call it your spiritual essence—or your psyche or inner being. You could even call it your soul.

What? You've lost touch with it? Then listen with all your other parts and perhaps you can get back in touch. Remember, you don't have to be religious to live an awakened life. It's yours to discover, free. What is an awakened life? It's having all of your "channels" open so that all messages—especially those you can't see or hear—are received. It's discovering the "you" in others and the "them" in you—discovering that your humanity lies beyond the boundaries of your body. It's finding and tapping into the invisible intelligence and power that lies in all forms.

And ultimately, it is discovering the power of your own thought and using it to create the life you want. Is all this possible? All this and more. You'll see it when you believe it, but belief must come first.

An important principle of living the awakened life is to "follow your bliss," as Joseph Campbell said. This means doing the things that make you truly happy—and not doing the things that bore or distress you. If you can't do what you love, you must learn to love what you do. One of the most difficult notions to give up is that you must continually strive for success and happiness. Once you discover the awakened life, you'll realize that success and happiness are not goals, they are by-products of your lifestyle.

The fact is, once you develop conscious contact with the spiritual nature of the universe—and once you allow yourself to live in harmony with it—big changes will occur.

This book was inspired by countless people over many, many years who have transformed their careers out of a desire to bring deeper meaning into their lives. I am blessed to have known some of these people, and I thank them for their uncompromising stamina in living up to their ideals and values—for they have made my own path easier.

For me, the process of opening myself to a more subtle reality began thirty-some years ago. I was facing an illness, and I had no idea what it was. Nor did I find out until six years ago. Now I know my discomfort was the work of a subtle force summoning me to a new and enchanted stage of life.

The first part of my life was spent following the expected paths, going along with others, imprisoning my spirit in order to be successful. But by withholding my true self, I had choked off my uniqueness. By following others, I had lost myself. My inner stirrings first appeared in the form of a real physical discomfort.

I'd get better and then worse. I'd be consumed with fear. I'd retreat and get better. Like a roller coaster, I was bouncing all over. And just when my life was starting to get better, I felt like things were getting worse—because for the first time I could see clearly what needed to be done. I always knew far more than I realized, but I didn't trust my inner knowing. Beyond the realm of daily life there is another quest—a journey up a mountain toward our hopes and dreams. This book serves as a map up that mountain and toward a new way of life—through the process of insight, discovery, and inspiration. This book is about courage, commitment, inner strength, a peaceful heart, self-trust, compassion, business, ethics, divorce, family, pain, and growth.

Libraries and bookstores offer information on every conceivable subject—facts, advice, and guidance about improving relationships, work, money, and health. Knowing what to do is not usually the problem. The elusive goal is translating intention into action and resolution into results. The gap between knowing and doing remains a weakness in most of our lives. We may resolve to improve our diet or exercise habits; we want to do it, we wish for the results, we even have a pretty good idea how to do it. But we wait for permission from our insides before we act. We want to feel motivated; we wait until fear, self-doubt, and insecurity dissolve. Nothing changes until we find the will to follow through. Our inner adversaries won't go away until we've faced them—until we do what feels right and necessary in spite of the fears or insecurities that may lurk within. When we come to love and accept ourselves, that love and acceptance will generate heroic efforts on our part—

and the commitment to stop destructive behavior and become masters of our destiny.

Positive change of any kind requires that we climb higher, expand our awareness, focus, pay attention, and invest time and energy. Those of us who master change—or at least accept it—recognize the cold, harsh realities. As Les Brown has said, "You know, we can't get out of life alive. We can either die in the bleachers or die on the field. We might as well come down on the field and go for it!"

In my own adventures, I've found that there is more to this world than meets the eye. Our lives are a mystery. So be gentle with yourself. Be as happy as you can be. Think less and feel more. And as you read this book, remember—we only have this moment.

So treat life like a dance rather than a wrestling match. Life rarely lays out a red carpet between you and your goals; more often, it's a swamp. But remember that your stumbling blocks can become stepping stones. And when life puts hurdles in your path, my friend, you had better become a hurdler.

Life:Wise and Wonderful

The only thing that stands between a man and what he wants from life is often merely the will to try it and the faith to believe that it is possible.

—Anonymous

CHAPTER 1

So you've got the career, the cars, the spouse, the spa, the house, the health club membership, the kids, the clothes. Trouble is, you're so frantic, frazzled, overbooked, and overwhelmed you don't have time to enjoy any of it.

Welcome to the hurried, harried ranks of those who suffer from the most dreaded disease of our age: the out-of-control (OOC) syndrome. OOC awaits for those high-achievers who burn themselves out acquiring other acronyms: MBA, CPA, J.D., M.D., PC, VCR, CD, IRA. "OOCs are people who are terribly busy, have very little free time, and feel that a lot of the tasks they take on to manage their lives are not getting done on time or at all," says Florence Skelly, president of a New York research firm. Ms. Skelly first diagnosed OOC in "single parents and two-earner households without children. They're getting up earlier and going to bed later—with their agendas constantly unfinished."

This phenomenon first entered the American culture in the eighties, and the epidemic shows no sign of abating. People continue to squeeze more activities into less time. Commuters are talking into their phones, dictating into tape recorders, eating breakfast, even reading newspapers while driving; they use errand services to pick up their dry cleaning or buy presents for their mothers. At health clubs you'll find people riding stationary cycles through lunch while scanning the sports page. At home, families rarely sit down to eat meals together, let alone cook them.

Why do OOCs do this to themselves? For some, the answer is necessity. "They work to pay rent or a mortgage, and to provide their kids with clothes and education and a few frills. The nature of the thing is if you're working forty hours a week at a job and you have kids, you're not going to have much time," says Diane Ulmer, executive director of Meyer Friedman Institute. Others take on more responsibilities to boost self-esteem. But in doing so we enter a vicious cycle. "We want more, and in the process we end up with less," says Nancy Ryan, a marriage and family therapist in San Jose, California. "Less quality in relationships with others. And less quality relationships with ourselves."

Our self-esteem is low so we say, "If I just had a new house, or lived in a better neighborhood, or had better clothes, then I'd be happy." It's easier to buy a new car to make you feel better than to find out who you are. The result: more work, less time for relationships, and a worsening case of the OOC syndrome.

Allow me to share a story about a friend who was living life in the fast lane—knee deep in the "American Dream" and definitely headed for OOC syndrome.

At midlife he was a successful marketing executive and owner of a small publishing company with fifteen employees. He had a house in the country, a place in the city, secretaries, lawyers, accountants, charge accounts—all that went with success. Yet he was a very miserable guy. That misery in the midst of plenty sent him off on a spiritual quest—not to some mountaintop in Tibet, but to find a way to be at peace with himself in everyday life. And his quest was successful. He became a full-time teacher of meditation and a much happier man.

There are other people besides my good friend who have made similar transformations. Each of their tales is unique—and describes a journey of transformation unlike any other. What they have in common is that each journey has been a spiritual one—not to some monastery in the Himilayas, but toward a deeper appreciation of the spiritual in everyday life.

But transformation does not refer to a single experience, something that happens once and leaves one permanently enlightened. It's an ongoing process, a never ending series of transformations.

My friend's story makes this point vividly. The route that led him from being a marketing executive to a teacher of Transcendental Meditation (TM) was not a direct or easy path, but a long and tortuous one. He describes his journey as a seemingly random series of influences that urged him to "turn to the silence and the power within."

He tells of how at odds his life was with his spirit during those days of climbing the corporate ladder. "My whole body rebelled against the lifestyle I had chosen," he says. "I was eating badly, sleeping badly, drinking too much, overworking. I had a bad case of colitis, ulceritis, and severe skin problems. I had OCC syndrome."

This crisis led my friend to the first of the major influences he credits with transforming his life. After seeing more than twenty doctors, he went to see a physician of naturopathy—someone who treats illness by using nutrition, exercise, vitamin and mineral supplements, and other natural elements. "I told him I had trunks full of pills, but still felt awful," my friend says.

But this physician said, "Oh, no problem, you'll be fine. You'll give up alcohol and coffee, and throw those cigarettes away." And he was so confident that my friend threw the cigarettes away, gave up three-martini lunches and coffee and danish, and before he knew it, every symptom disappeared, and he regained his energy.

A second formative experience for my friend was more spiritual. He was in his forties at the time, and deeply depressed. He tried various kinds of therapy, then one day as he prepared for a skiing trip in Europe, a colleague suggested he visit a German Zen master. The meeting changed my friend's life...again. He ended up staying ten days in Zurich, where the Zen master taught him deep breathing and coached him on becoming present. "What he was trying to say was that life is in the moment," said my friend. "Somehow that got into me and I began to experiment, walking in the woods, feeling the trees and the earth below me. When you start feeling that, your hair stands on end."

When my friend got home, his wife hardly recognized him. "My face looked totally different," my friend said. "It was no longer guarded but open." He went back to his business refreshed. Over the following month, however, the anxiety began to come back. It was much later before he was to undergo a much more enduring transformation.

It began innocently enough. One day he accompanied his son to a lecture on TM—and snickered at some of what he heard. "We're living with nine thousand vibratory negatives in our lives, and Maharishi Mahesh Yogi says, 'Close your eyes for twenty minutes and you're going to achieve a state of purity.' It took me years to understand what he meant was that gradually everything in your life begins to change because you feel a sense of orderliness, just a touch of it. And without realizing it, your life has changed dramatically. There's more room for understanding your limitations and the limitations of others."

After doing the work at home for eighteen months, my friend was convinced. He resigned from his marketing job, sold his small publishing business, and took a year of study to become accredited as a teacher of TM. Ultimately he became part of its inner circle.

He sees his path now as one of helping others. "I don't believe that you purify your own system and stop there," he says. "This instrument that you've been developing is ultimately for the purpose of doing for others."

■ Learning to Love the Plateau

Early in life we are urged to study hard to get good grades. We are told to get good grades so that we can graduate from high school and get into college so we can get a good job. We are compelled to get a good job so that we can buy a house and a car. Again and again, we are told to do one thing so that we can get something else. We spend our lives stretched on a rack of contingencies.

No question, contingencies are important. The achievement of goals is important. But the real juice of life, bitter or sweet, is found less in the product of our efforts than in the process—in life itself, and how it feels to be alive. We are taught in countless ways to value the product, the prize. But if our life is a good one, most of it will be spent on a plateau—in the process of achievement. And nowhere in our upbringing, our schooling, our careers, are we taught to appreciate, to value, to enjoy, even to love the plateau.

I was fortunate, in my early thirties, to have discovered running—a discipline so resistant to the quick fix that it showed me the plateau in sharp, bold relief. When I started running, I assumed that I would steadily improve. My early plateaus were relatively short in duration, and I could ignore them easily. After about a year and a half, however, I was forced to recognize that I was on a plateau of rather formidable proportions. This caused a certain amount of shock and disappointment, but somehow I persevered and finally experienced an apparent spurt of improvement. The next time my forward progress stopped, I said to myself, "Oh, shoot. Another plateau." After a few more months there was another spurt of progress, and then, of course, the inevitable plateau. But this time, something marvelous happened. I found myself thinking, "Oh boy. Another plateau. Good. I can just stay on it and keep on practicing. Sooner or later, there'll be another spurt. But actually, that doesn't even matter." It was one of the warmest moments on my journey.

To be sure, goals and contingencies are important. But they exist in the future and the past, beyond the pale of the sensory realm. Practice, the path of mastery, exists only in the present. You can see it, hear it, smell it, feel it. To love the plateau is to love the eternal now—enjoy the spurts of progress and the fruits of accomplishment as they occur, then accept serenely the plateau that lies just beyond them. To love the plateau is to love what is most essential and enduring in your life.

▪

Traverse

How easy it is to insulate ourselves from ourselves.

How easy it is to get lost in our daily tribulations.
So convenient are they to keep us distracted from the task at hand.

Can our egos not withstand a moment of silent scrutiny?

A glimpse of the rawness we dress with propriety...Can the beauty
of ourselves remain hidden from the fear of traversing the
wood of darkness? From inward comes life, as a child from its
mother, the butterfly from the cocoon. From inward comes the
splendor of the flower, the moisture from the sky.

From inward comes your true reality, the magnificence of you.

—Aurora C. Gonzalez

▪

▪ Rules for Being Human

I did not create these rules. They come from an unknown source, which I acknowledge with gratitude.

1. You will receive a body. You may like it or hate it, but it will be yours for the duration.

2. You will learn lessons. You are enrolled in a full-time (but informal) school called life. Each day you will have the opportunity to learn lessons. You may like the lessons or think them irrelevant or stupid.

3. There are no mistakes, only lessons. Growth is a process of trial and error—of experimentation. The "failed" experiments are as much a part of the process as the experiment that ultimately "works."

4. A lesson is repeated until it is learned. A lesson will be presented to you in various forms until you have learned it. Then you can go on to the next lesson.

5. There is no end to learning. There is no part of life that does not contain its lessons. If you are alive, there are lessons to be learned.

6. "There" is no better than "here." When your "there" has become a "here," you will simply obtain another "there" which, again, will look better than "here."

7. Others are merely mirrors of youself. You cannot love or hate something about another person unless it reflects to you something that you love or hate about yourself.

8. What you make of your life is up to you. You have all the tools and resources you need. What you do with them is up to you.

9. The answers lie inside of you. All you need to do is look, listen, and trust.

-

A Creed to Live By

Don't undermine your worth by comparing yourself with others.
It is because we are different that each of us is special. Don't set
your goals by what others deem important. Only you know
what's best for you.

Don't take for granted the things closest to your heart.
Cling to them as you would your life, for without them life is
meaningless. Don't give up when you still have something to give.
Nothing is really over ... until the moment you stop trying.
Don't be afraid to admit that you are less than perfect. It is

*this fragile thread that binds us to each other. Don't be afraid
to confront risks. It is by taking chances that we learn how to
be brave. Don't shut love out of your life by saying it's impossible
to find. The quickest way to lose love is to hold it too tightly;
and the best way to keep it is to give it wings.*

*Don't dismiss your dreams. To be without dreams is to be
without hope. To be without hope is to be without purpose.
Don't run through life so fast that you forget not only where you've
been, but where you are going. Life is not a race, but a journey to
be savored each step of the way.*

—Nancy Sims

▄ Taking Time for Life

As I write this, it is shortly before Labor Day weekend—the American ritual that marks the end of summer. Notions of work and leisure are very much in the air. I myself started recovering this summer from a twenty-year bout with workaholism.

And then there's Joe. He's an old friend who took it into his head two years ago simply to quit working. Formerly a well-paid statistician, Joe now lives in a house on the Missouri River. He plays all day: building a string maze in the forest (The Amazing Mazomanic Maze, he calls it), amusing himself with fractal equations on his computer, and writing a historical brochure about the river. But I suspect that mostly Joe sleeps late and walks around the woods. His partner, Martha, provides the financial support. Joe did the same for her while she was in school, so he figures it's his turn now.

I saw Joe not long ago. I stepped out of my own harried existence into his lazy world. One morning we had a long talk over breakfast about things that have since stayed on my mind—about what slaves we are to work, and how it's possible to live our lives another way if we set our minds to it.

But change isn't easy, and what Joe did is almost inconceivable to me—to most of us, I imagine. Joe has taken two years off—while I feel guilty for an occasional early departure from the office. Something in us militates against genuine leisure. We seem to resent leisure as an intrusion upon the sacred truth that work is the substance of life.

Think, for example, about George Bush's adamant vacationing in the midst of the Kuwait crisis. It looked bad, journalists said, for Bush to run around the golf course when Saddam Hussein had the world on the edge of war. But in the next breath, the same journalists applauded Bush's "near flawless" handling of the crisis.

I, for one, wonder whether one might have something to do with the other. Whether a relaxed mind might be less likely to come up with an agitated and imprudent response. Whether better decisions might naturally emerge from a leisurely setting, rather than a formal and austere one.

Psychologists might agree on the abstract truth of the benefit of leisure. But the truth is that our culture can't even comfortably give permission to the President of the United States to relax, so convinced are we that leisure is frivolous. "The American chintziness about vacations is absurd," observes Michael Kinsley in an August 1990 edition of *Time*. Recalling a stint he did with the *Economist* in London, Kinsley notes that employees there routinely take five weeks of vacation each year, plus two weeks at Christmas and another two at Easter. The French get five weeks vacation by law; the Germans get six.

Even when we grant the necessity of leisure in our culture, we tend to justify it in terms of work. We don't say, "Vacation is fun." We justify, "Vacation leaves me less stressed and better able to focus on work." We don't say, "Overtime is unpleasant because there's so much more to life." We rationalize, "Productivity drops after forty hours." Business journalism justifies every humane action a company takes in terms of economics. But I suspect I'll wait in vain for the day the *Wall Street Journal* reports that a company opened an employee gymnasium for no good reason at all.

When did work become our master? American culture today tends to look back at the Victorians as overly rigid and stern, but what about us? We who often think taking a nap is as radical an act as the Boston Tea Party. What's at work here, I think, has to do with self-esteem—our personal esteem and the esteem of our culture as "the most advanced on earth."

There's a theory that there are two kinds of self-esteem. One is based on efficacy—the ability to get things done in the world. The other is based simply upon being okay, no matter what we can or cannot do. Our culture values the former at the expense of the latter.

I know I'm personally caught in the efficacy trap. When I'm not working hard—especially on those weekdays when I'm not really working at all—I feel listless and not good for much. Sometimes I ask myself, "What am I trying to prove and to whom?" It's as though I'm trying to earn a right to exist, as though my life is an imperiled right, easily lost through inactivity.

The virtue of our work ethic is in how important being productive makes us feel, how valuable our output assures us we are. I remember fighting with one of my senior executives one morning, working furiously the rest of the day, and being reluctant to leave the office that evening. The calmness outside my window somehow seemed frightening.

The quiet and calm of daily existence is a time of coming back to our fundamental self—the self we were in childhood and will be again in old age, the self we are every evening, the self without the title, or business suit, or mask. Daily existence is a time of coming down from the urgent and self-important stratosphere of business to put our feet back on earth.

To loosen the stranglehold work has on our lives, perhaps we need most of all to connect with our own humility and to remember our birthright: the simple way we belong on the earth, the way all creatures do, in a way we need not earn. We do not have to prove our worth to anyone, but simply embrace it as one embraces a warm summer day.

■ Mythical Standards of Success

Television and other seductive media lead us to some very suspect beliefs. We come to think of certain things as universal. For example, being the best has come to mean there is a standard out there that all of us must meet if we want to be winners.

The media tell us life is a big game show, and the prizes we all shoot for include instant name recognition, wealth, constant happiness, youthful vitality, and beauty. These mythical standards of success are spreading like cancer throughout our culture. We need only look at the preoccupation with material wealth to realize we are in real danger.

Ads fail to explain that we can't drink, inhale, or snort happiness. For when we look at life wisely, we know we can't buy happiness, eat it, drive it, live in it, or travel to it. Happiness is the journey, not the destination. Happiness is rooted in the inner self—in living life. Happiness is not the outer trappings, the items we own or acquire, in the positions we gain and the kudos we receive.

■ The Drama of Life

I am a spectator at the drama of my life. I'm also the writer, producer, director, and star. Everyone I know is a supporting character in my play—even a co-star of this scene or that. Even those I meet briefly or casually have a role as walk-ons or extras. The play is always fascinating, for I seldom know just what I'll do or how the other actors will respond.

When I take this view, I get a better sense of what my life looks like from the outside. Times of tragedy begin to be exactly that—dramatic scenes to be known and fully experienced—rather than seeming like the end of everything, to be escaped at any cost.

Were my play nothing but peaches and cream, I would be shallow and dull. My struggles, my hard decisions, and the painful events I have lived through are important learning experiences. My drama has scenes of comedy and scenes of tragedy. Both are a part of who I am.

Each supporting character in my play is also the star of his or her own show. And just as those people are minor characters in my play, I am a minor character in theirs. I can appreciate their drama just as I appreciate my own. I can simply be silent and watch another person's play for a while, appreciating it without judging. As a result, I'm less locked into my own viewpoints. And I can more easily understand another person's way of experiencing the world.

■ Are We a Society of Hedgers?

One of my primary sources of irritation with today's world is society's tendency to hedge all actions so that no one ever has to say that he or she is wrong.

On the way home from the office several months ago, I listened to a radio interview with a football coach as his team was preparing to take the field. The sportscaster asked, "Coach, this is a big game tonight. Are you going to win?" The coach replied, "Well, you know we're going to give it the best we've got."

"You don't sound too confident, Coach," commented the interviewer. "Oh, we have a positive attitude, and we are going to play our best," drawled the coach.

The interview lasted five minutes, and not once did the coach answer a question directly, nor did he ever say, "We are going to win!" After listening to the interview, I felt the coach did not have confidence in himself or his team, and that he was afraid to take a winning stand.

Coaches are not the only ones who hedge their statements. The trend pervades all areas of society. A few weeks ago I was in a conference room discussing how a friend of mine would defend himself against a lawsuit. The amount of money involved was huge, but my friend saw little merit in the charge, just a big chance for his accuser to get publicity. My friend asked the chief defense lawyer what he thought of the suit.

He replied, "I haven't had a chance to study the case in all its aspects, but it does seem they drafted the complaint with the hope of getting some publicity."

My friend was rather upset. "What do you mean that you haven't had a chance to study the suit? We are going into the deposition."

The lawyer smiled. "I didn't say I wasn't prepared. I said I hadn't had a chance to study the case. We don't have any discovery yet, so I don't know what they have."

My friend became livid. "What have you been doing for the last three months? You must have some estimate of our chances."

The lawyer shifted in his chair, took off his glasses, and started to hedge. "We can't tell about suits like this. Judges are strange people—they tend to protect the little guy. There are too many unknowns at this point, so I can't give you an opinion as to our chances. We will give it all we've got."

Have you ever read a loan commitment or a letter of intent to finance from an investment banking house? They contain so many escape clauses that you wonder whether it is necessary to have the "commitment" in writing. We have developed a society of hedgers. Where is our pioneer drive, the confidence that built this country? Can you believe America was settled by positive achievement? When I was a kid, we were taught to say, "Yes, I can. Yes, I will." Today, you more often hear, "Maybe ... if ... we'll see."

It seems to me that if you are going to make something happen, you must be certain that you can accomplish the objective and you must be willing to say so out loud. A few years ago, Mohammad Ali would call the round in which he was going to knock out his opponent. And frequently he would accomplish this goal exactly on cue. He didn't say, "I hope I can win" or "My opponent is good, but I'm going to give it all I've got." He said, "I'm going to whup him in the third round" and "I'm the greatest." And he was!

I don't believe a coach can lead a team to the championship by fostering an attitude of "just give it your best." I don't believe anyone can win a lawsuit armed with only an analytical approach. You have to believe with all your heart and soul that you are going to win. I am aware that legally there must be contingencies and loopholes in financial commitments, but the ho-hum attitude that accompanies the hedging disgusts me.

I don't know who started this trend, but I don't like it.

■ The Big Power in Little Ideas

Here are three things I know about ideas in the workplace:

- ■ Little ideas get little respect.

- Big ideas get all the attention and applause and resources.
- The best ideas usually start out as little ideas and grow into big ideas.

I jotted these three thoughts on a yellow pad the other day as I listened to a silver-tongued venture capitalist outline his latest brainstorm. He was looking for investors in a concept that would revolutionize how Americans shop. There was no doubt that the idea was grand and ambitious, and had the potential to be hugely profitable if it worked. It also required a tremendous amount of up-front investment.

That's when I scribbled my three bullet points. I did it to remind myself of the seductive power of big ideas. They lure you in with their cleverness, their originality, their sweeping vision and dramatic scope—and not incidentally, their promise of big returns. But more often than not, big ideas are a mirage. They take an inordinate amount of energy and manpower and money to keep them moving along successfully—and if any of those ingredients disappears for a moment, the big idea can come to a grinding halt.

In reality, the best ideas rarely start out as big ideas. They tend to start out small.

The irony, however, is that there is little motivation in the workplace for people to come up with little ideas. Every reward structure in the workplace, whether it's tangible or psychic, encourages us to wrap our ideas in as big and impressive a package as possible. The big idea draws attention to us. It lets us stand out from the crowd. It brands us as bold, innovative thinkers. And it puts a big chunk of the company's resources under our control. After all, a big agenda requires a big investment.

And yet, everything in my experience convinces me that the best ideas show up at your door in little packages.

■ Sparring in the Ring of Life

When we get up each day, we step into the ring with the challenges of daily life—not only the external challenges of other people and tasks, but the inner battles with fear, insecurity, jealousy, envy, and self-doubt.

Life comforts the disturbed and disturbs the comfortable. Sometimes, out of nowhere, life lands a left hook that really shakes us up; we get slammed into the ropes, or knocked to the canvas. Maybe the shock comes in the form of a financial crisis, a death in the family, a divorce, or an illness or injury.

Such stresses can shock and disorient us, but they also wake us from our comfortable slumber and catalyze our subconscious into generating the energy and focus we need to make life changes. They can expand our reference point so we ask ourselves: What is my life for? Who am I? Where have I been and where am I headed?

When we get broadsided by circumstances—if life lands a one-two punch and knocks us to the canvas—we can stay down or we can stand up. Standing up after a bad fall can require great effort and courage. When we finally get back on our feet, we can look our adversary in the eye, put our hands on our hips, and say, "Okay, you knocked me down, but I got up, and I'm going to keep getting up." You can sum up a warrior's attitude toward adversity with the words, "Was that your best shot? C'mon, give me your *best shot!*"

■ Don't Be a Grudge Collector

Too many people spend too much time thinking of past hurts, suffered through office politics, messed-up relationships, and the evils of the world in general. Don't waste your energy this way. Rather, apply your mind to forgiving and forgetting. Think positive and pleasing thoughts.

Many people believe Norman Vincent Peale was the originator of positive thinking. But Dr. Peale, a minister for some fifty years, would tell you the Apostle Paul was way ahead of him. In the first century A.D., Paul wrote, "Whatever things are true, whatever things are noble, whatever things are lovely, whatever things are of good report, if there is any virtue, and if there is anything praiseworthy—meditate on these things."

Don't brag. Attention seekers need constant approval. Have the quiet confidence to let your actions speak for you. When you have real value, you don't have to flaunt an imitation.

Get high on doing good. No one in history has found lasting satisfaction in chemicals and possessions. Real pleasure comes from good work, generous deeds, and grateful thoughts.

Don't give in to ads and fads. Look for and listen to the truth. Rather than hear what you want to hear, listen for the facts of the matter under consideration. Everything you think is only your opinion, based on impressions from limited input. Always consider the source and credibility of your value system.

Wake up happy. Optimism is a learned attitude. (So is pessimism, so why not learn something that will help you?) Start thinking positively early in the day. If the alarm sets your nerves jangling, wake up to music instead. I strongly advise avoiding the morning news. It's almost always depressing. Listen instead to an all-music radio station or your favorite cassettes on your way to work.

Find a positive support group. Get involved with some positive peers who meet at least once a month for lunch or after work to discuss and brainstorm ways to achieve goals. Support groups that give me the most help include people from different ethnic groups, different lifestyles, and different philosophies and viewpoints. At the same time, I never share my problems with people who can't give me positive suggestions and direct me toward solutions. I always seek an optimistic, divergent, or different approach that inspires my creativity and imagination.

Above all, make every day and every evening the best possible. Once spent, they are gone forever. Invested in creatively, they bring a return much higher than any interest rate ever will. Your attitude is either the lock on the door to real self-esteem and being the best you can be, or it is the key that will open you up to more and more joyous moments in life.

■ Develop Ongoing Gratitude

A strong, perpetual sense of gratitude strengthens the bond between you and life's riches. I'm not speaking of the occasional "thank you" muttered heavenward when something good comes your way. Rather, you must actively cultivate a reverent conviction that allows you to focus exclusively upon your positive ideal without inner conflict or guilt.

Being grateful for life's blessings presupposes the realization of your ideal and compels you to keep your success foremost in your thoughts. Thus, gratitude helps you to transcend negative thoughts and recognize that every person and experience has some value for you.

So set aside a few minutes each morning before getting out of bed to reflect upon the good things in your life. Give thanks for your health, your friends and family, and the continual learning opportunities afforded you by life.

■ Another Birthday, So What?

I can no longer put off facing all of the thorny or perplexing or tedious situations that my resolutions are intended to address. Each birthday I've been full of resolve as I face new challenges, new situations. But often as not, I find myself struggling with the same issues I was dealing with the year before. Sound familiar?

I've figured out that change in itself doesn't do much to "fix" my life. New circumstances have rarely brought the thrill I'd hoped they would. So what does it take to effect change that really matters? What does it take not just to alter surface appearance, but to shift the very ground on which I stand?

I've spent most of my life in search of answers. I have a problem and I want a solution. I have a dilemma and I want a guarantee that I'll make the right choice. I have little patience for uncertainty, for unresolved tension. Instead of asking new questions, I want the information that resolves those I already have and forestalls any that might arise.

But the times when I've been truly creative—when I've been the boldest and most imaginative, when I've taken the lead—have been those times *when I was willing not to know.* They were times not of certainty, but of wonder. Times when the ready answer was insufficient to meet my commitments. When I had to ask new questions to handle the challenges ahead. They were times when I was willing to risk what I knew for what I might learn. Times of openness, of inquiry, of excitement at discovering the vast possibilities that life presents.

Now I'm on my way from vision to action. I'm exploring new horizons, posing new questions, accepting new challenges, opening new doors. In doing so, I'm rekindling the boundless excitement of living, renewing that sense of amazement and delight that lends a sparkle and vitality to even the most ordinary of events. As never before, I'm committed to meeting life with energy and vigor, and to tackling the adventure of living with gusto.

∎

When I Am an Old Woman

I shall wear purple
With a red hat which doesn't go, and doesn't suit me,
And I shall spend my pension on brandy and summer gloves, and
satin sandals,
And say we've no money for butter.
I shall sit down on the pavement when I'm tired
And gobble up samples in shops and press alarm bells
And run my stick

Along the public railings
And make up for the sobriety of my youth.

I shall go out in slippers in the rain
And pick the flowers
In other people's gardens, and learn to spit.

You can wear terrible shirts and grow more fat
And eat three pounds of sausages at a go
Or only bread and a pickle for a week
And hoard pens and pencils and beermats and things in boxes.

But now we must have clothes that keep us dry
And pay our rent
And not swear in the street, and set a good example for
the children.

We will have friends to dinner and read the papers.

But maybe I ought to practice a little now?

So people who know me
are not too shocked and surprised when suddenly I am old and
start to wear purple.

—Author unknown

■ Five Keys to Successful Living

The capacity to love. Not just romance is needed for longevity. You also need genuine caring and concern for other people. It's important to reach out a helping hand, to give of yourself, to do just a little more. Love, as the song says, makes the world go round—and it also binds people together.

The capacity to learn—from books, from experiences, from the world around you. Learning has to be a lifelong process because changes come so rapidly. An open mind, ready and eager to absorb each new bit of knowledge, is an asset worth cultivating.

The capacity to labor. There are times when a life of ease can seem very appealing—nothing to do but relax and enjoy the world around you. Actually, though, it's work—on the job, at home, in a volunteer situation—that provides the real rewards. The sense of satisfaction when you finish a big project, for example, the feeling of pride when you solve a particularly sticky problem—these are life's subtle rewards.

The capacity to laugh—at yourself as well as at others. Life can sometimes be hard, dreary. The capacity to see the humor in certain situations, to enjoy the funny side of life, can brighten not only your day but that of the people around you.

The capacity to leave. We all have people and things that we care about very strongly. But the day may come when they are no longer part of our lives. A loved one departs, a good job is lost, a valued situation changes for one reason or another. When that time comes, a period of grieving is in order, but it should soon be set aside. The past is over and done with—it's time to move ahead.

On first reading, these may seem like simple qualities that exist to some degree in all of us. But it's in applying and sustaining them that truly successful living occurs.

■ Healthy Pleasures

Imagine the world without pleasure. Life would appear colorless and humorless. A baby's smile would go unappreciated. Foods would be tasteless. The beauty of a Bach concerto would fall on deaf ears. Joy, thrills, delights, ecstasy, elation, and happiness would disappear. The touch of a mother would not soothe, and a lover could not arouse. Interest in sex and procreation would dry up. The next generation would wait unborn.

Human beings evolved to seek enjoyment to enhance survival. What better way to assure that healthy, life-saving behaviors occur than to make them pleasurable? From eating to reproduction, from attending to the environment to caring for others, pleasure guides us to better health. Doing what feels right and feeling good are usually beneficial for health and the survival of the species.

Yet at nearly every turn, pleasure has gotten a bad name. People are almost phobic about having fun, increasingly viewing themselves as fragile, vulnerable, ready to develop cancer or heart disease at the slightest provocation. In the name of health, people give up many of their life enjoyments. Compulsion, disruption, and disease lurk if we lapse. Research and thinking in medicine and psychology reflect this pathological focus on the causes and treatment of disease, while virtually ignoring acts that build health. There is a strong anti-pleasure bias in medical research, with a great amount of information about the health hazards of pleasure and little about its health-promoting effects.

There are many more studies of the disastrous repercussions of lifelong alcoholism than research about the benefits of moderate alcohol consumption. There are myriad studies about noise exposure but hardly a score on the therapeutic benefits of music. Researchers dwell on sexual dysfunction and the lethal dangers of sexually transmitted diseases; they catalog thousands of sexual aberrations. But they spell out little on how a pleasurable sex life contributes to well-being. We have to move beyond "Just Say No" to some positive messages about satisfying ways to improve health.

Don't get me wrong. We recognize that exercising, not smoking or drinking to excess, wearing seatbelts, avoiding extreme sunburn, and other cautious behavior all contribute to a long, healthy life. Even so, the sum total of all the "good health habits" still doesn't add up to as much as we might believe and doesn't explain the essential vitality of some people.

We have no quarrel with the evidence that some pleasures, like cigarette smoking, high alcohol consumption, addictive drugs, and driving recklessly, are unhealthy and should be knocked off, whether you fancy them or not. Clearly, some pleasures and some conditions are injurious to health. And some pleasures can become addictive compulsions, destroying lives, relationships, and pleasure itself.

The important thing is that worrying too much about anything—including calories, salt, cancer, and cholesterol—can rob your life of vitality, and that living optimistically, with pleasure, zest, and commitment, enriches if not lengthens life.

■ Life Insurance: Our Seventy-Year Warranty

We are born with a seventy-year warranty, but few of us read the instructions. We go blindly through life without consulting a manual for the operation of the human machine. The maintenance and preservation of our bodies doesn't seem to concern us. Many act as if longevity and freedom from malfunction have been built in by the Creator.

They have. But only if we take care of our bodies as we would our cars. We have to follow certain rules to get maximum longevity out of what we were given at birth. We have to use the biological wisdom gained over the centuries to guide our day-to-day living. Make no mistake about this. Nature does not allow for error, and she is not reluctant to inflict capital punishment. Deviations from the correct regimen can shorten one's days. Aging is inexorable. Death is inevitable. But neither should occur before their appointed time. Individual behavior determines individual health. We can choose to avoid unnecessary illness and premature death. We can decide to be active or sedentary. To age quickly or slowly. To die before or after our time.

■ It Could Be Worse

Sometimes things go from bad to worse; sometimes the light at the end of the tunnel turns out to be the headlight of an oncoming train.

Pete went to his doctor for a complete physical examination. The doctor called him a few days later and said, "The lab reports are in; I have bad news and I have worse news."

Confused and troubled, Pete said, "Bad news and worse news? Well, what's the bad news?"

"You have twenty-four hours to live," the doctor informed him. "The lab reports are conclusive."

In shock, Peter could only say, "Twenty-four hours? But what's the worse news?"

"Oh, that," the doctor answered casually. "I meant to call you yesterday."

—Anonymous

■ The Alameda Seven

In the early seventies, Americans thought that a balanced diet, a good night's sleep, and regular visits to the family physician would assure health. Around the same time, we learned several rules for a longer, healthier (and hence more productive) life from the long-lived, happy people of Alameda County, California. They are known as the Alameda Seven:

1. Exercise regularly.
2. Eat a good breakfast.
3. Don't eat between meals.
4. Maintain age-25 weight.
5. Don't smoke.

6. Drink moderately.

7. Get a good night's sleep.

These guidelines have stood the test of subsequent scientific investigation. People who follow six of them live significantly longer and have fewer hospital admissions than those who follow only one or two.

We aim not only for a long life, but for one free of incapacitating disease. We want to avoid illness, to be sick as little as possible. We would like to live a fully functioning life until the last possible moment. And people who live by the Alameda Seven will apparently do that as well. A 1984 study showed that those who observed the rules remained in an independent, highly functional state of health beyond the age of seventy.

How best to live long and live well? Start by following the Alameda Seven. You will live until you are seventy years old, and you will function well while you are doing so. But what of delving deeper into the intricacies of aging and performance? The secrets of past generations are there for our perusal. We can learn much from discovering them for ourselves, rather than waiting for some scientist to do so for us. For past generations, lifestyle was the leading health factor. People then had no antibiotics, no cures for infectious disease. They had to rely on their manner of living to preserve their health.

Now we have grown soft. Free, for the most part, from the scourges of pneumonia and tuberculosis and other life-shortening diseases, our longevity may be increasing, but so are the diseases born of the way we live. We die from the affluence and the sedentary life that prosperity has given us. If we are indeed to prosper, we must look to the rules of the generations that preceded us and had to struggle for existence—people who read the warranty and followed it.

■

Pearls of Wisdom

You may not have been responsible for your heritage, but you are responsible for your future.

If you want to know what your mind was like in the past, examine your body now. If you want to know what your life will be like in the future, examine your mind now.

—Deepak Chopra

■

There's always room for improvement. It's the biggest room in the house.

—Louise Heath Leber

We never know what ripples of healing we set in motion by simply smiling on one another.

—Henry Drummond

Desire joy and thank God for it. Renounce it, if need be, for others' sake. That's joy beyond joy.

—Robert Browning

There is no duty we underrate as much as the duty of being happy.

—Robert Louis Stevenson

We can be lost in cosmic bliss, and still be responsible for remembering our zip code.

—Ram Dass

Life should be gulped not sipped.

—Unknown

■ Personal Truths of Joseph Campbell

But whether small or great, and no matter what the stage or grade of life, the call rings up the curtain, always, on a mystery of transfiguration—a rite, or moment, of spiritual passage, which, when complete, amounts to a dying and a birth. The familiar life horizon has been outgrown; the old concepts, ideals, and emotional patterns no longer fit; the time for the passing of a threshold is at hand.

—from *The Hero with a Thousand Faces*

Success

—

The job is, if we are willing to take it seriously, to help ourselves to be more perfectly what we are, to be more full, more actualizing, more realizing, in fact, what we are in potentiality.

—*Abraham Maslow*

CHAPTER 2

Success is a very personal thing, meaning something different to each of us. To ninety-five percent of the families on earth, success is having land to till—or any job that pays and a way to earn enough to provide nourishment for their children to grow in decent health into adulthood. Success in America is usually associated with material wealth, fame, and/or social status. Maybe this definition needs rethinking. I suggest here that it is not what one gets that makes one successful, but what one does with what one has.

We Americans often dream of gaining success and then sitting back to enjoy it like a giant lollipop that never melts away. However, true happiness and fulfillment seem to be associated with the richness of the journey, not with the fleeting moment of having arrived. Success is not a destination; it is a way to travel. And the road to success is always under construction.

To feel successful deep inside, we need to understand why we were created, who we are, and what we really want in life. A feeling of inner joy and success is harder to acquire than a Mercedes, a vice presidency, or a castle with a wine cellar. A wealthy, happy, and successful real-estate broker confided to me that he could have made more money in his life, but he preferred to sleep well at night. This broker had found life's ideal combination—outer as well as inner success. He stumbled onto the secret when he realized that all success must be built from the inside out.

Sleeping well after a good day at honest work is one of the joys of life. People who can't find peace in their own beds often seek it on the psychiatrist's couch. The disciples of Freud and Jung grow rich counseling individuals who cannot enjoy what they have earned. In fact, many of today's "most successful" people continue to travel from therapist to guru, from cult hero to fad book, trying to discover some joy in life. With all their outer trappings, they carry the heavy burden of emptiness.

People who play the comparison game are immediately vulnerable to feelings of frustration and unworthiness. When they see others who are smarter, younger, more clever, or better looking, their automatic conclusion is that these others are better than they are and deserve better things in life. As we have learned, the success of others has little to do with our own personal success. True success is not measured by what others may say or accomplish. Although we tend to compare ourselves to others, the happiest folks know that they don't really compete. Their success comes from doing *their* best, based on their own unique skills and talents.

Instead of achieving or performing to impress the world or your peers, seek to do something that is beautiful, excellent, and heartwarming. Suppose, for example, that you learn a certain piece on the piano. You practice long and hard on a difficult concerto, and then you are ready to perform. You may play the piece for one person or for hundreds, but the size of the audience isn't the reason you sought to master the music. You did it for the sheer exhilaration of doing your best. You need no one else to measure you or your skill. Your gallery is God and your own self-respect.

It is futile to seek success in one magnificent package perched at the top of a mountain. Nothing lasting or satisfying is up there. Real success comes in small portions day by day—a smile, a hug, a sunset, sand between your toes, a satisfied customer, a child's happy squeal, the smell of lilacs, a hand extended, a phone call from a friend, a flowering tree, a tasty meal eaten without haste. The list is endless, but our minutes to enjoy and appreciate life's small successes are not. If there is one thing I want my children to learn from me, it is to take pleasure in life's little daily treasures. This is the most important thing I have discovered about measuring success.

And remember, it is not all that difficult to be a five-star person. Start with your God-given inner value ... that's first. Add the self-respect that comes from absolute and uncompromising integrity. Add purpose beyond yourself, blend in discipline, and follow up with graciousness. This is the recipe for being a five-star person. Being the best is no more and no less than doing the best, giving the best, in everything you do.

■ How to Lead the Pack

How do you instantly convert yourself from being just another commodity to leading your field as its most distinctive, proprietary business? The answer is surprisingly easy. Here are the "magic" steps to take:

First: Start seeing yourself as a value creator—someone whose company and product provide or add tremendous value to your customer's life or business. Then start consciously focusing on the increased quality of life or business your customer enjoys when he or she does business with your firm, and fully benefits from the advantage your product provides.

Next: Stop seeing your business as a vehicle to make money with or from. Instead, view it as a perpetual machine for making people's lives better.

Next: Add more to what you do than your competitors offer—more attention, more education, more service, technical support, bonuses, warranties, and communication.

Next: Make a list—a long, comprehensive list—of all the ways you could innovate with your people, products, or perspectives ... if you had the time, money, and staff to do it.

Next: Ask yourself: Why wait for all three of these? Start doing every innovation on your list that doesn't require a lot more expense or people. But don't just go about it halfheartedly. Give it your all—put passion, purpose, and priority into your efforts.

Also, don't do things intermittently—do them formally, strategically, and continuously, as if your life depended on your executing them continuously and successfully.

Next: Start thinking about how much more is possible—how much more you could be doing with your time, your opportunities, your efforts. Don't get frustrated, get motivated to put more accomplishment into everything that everyone in your organization does—including you.

Next: Review my 11 Strategic Pillars of Enduring Business Success.

1. Continuously identifying and discovering hidden assets in your business.

2. Mining cash-windfall each and every month out of your business.

3. Engineering success into every action you take and every decision you make.

4. Building your business on a foundation of multiple profit sources, instead of depending on a single revenue source.

5. Being different, special, and unique, and demonstrating an advantage in the eyes of your customers.

6. Creating real value for your customers and employees for maximum loyalty and results.

7. Gaining the maximum personal leverage from every action, investment, and time or energy commitment you make.

8. Networking/masterminding/brainstorming with like-minded, success-driven people who share real life experiences with you.

9. Turning yourself into an idea generator and recognized innovator within your industry or market.

10. Making "growth thinking" part of your everyday business philosophy.

11. Reversing the risk for both you and your clients/customers in everything you do (so the downside is almost zero and the upside potential nearly infinite). Do this by using small, safe tests to eliminate dangerous risks and by adopting funnel vision instead of tunnel vision in your thinking.

Then: Resolve that your business, your people, your prospects, your purpose, and your possibilities will always be superior, in all categories, to those of your competitors.

Resolve: To change the game you are playing in business—as well as the rules you are playing by: Play to win, but play at a level of integrity and complete advantage that your business adversaries can't possibly equal.

Finally: Have a ball in the process. Business can and should be enjoyable and fun if played properly—more fun, in fact, than most other recreational alternatives.

■ The Seven Laws of Success

There are four main reasons people are unsuccessful in attaining their goals: negative attitudes, procrastination, ignorance about money and success, and failure to set goals. Here are some tips to develop your success strategy.

Law 1: Clearing

Nature abhors a vacuum. When you clear out the clutter in your life, something else will fill up the space. Make a list of anything you would be willing to toss out: old clothes, outdated magazines, duplicates, obsolete notebooks. Throw out whatever you no longer use.

It takes faith and trust to complete this housecleaning. For example, I clean out my files when business slows down, and the phone inevitably rings with offers of new business. The process works, but you have to take a risk.

Law 2: Giving

When we give, we begin the flow of receiving. The old expression does apply: What goes around, comes around. Whatever we give out seems to come back to us. In sales, I appreciate getting leads from others, and I receive a good many of them because I return the favor. I often refer potential customers to someone else if they could better service an account.

Law 3: Excelling

Everyone has the potential for success. Some people undermine their own possibilities because they don't believe they deserve good things in their lives. I have used the following rules to increase my self-esteem and attract more success:

■ Love yourself 100 percent. This means all of you ... your assets and your liabilities.

■ Acknowledge your uniqueness and use your special talents.

■ Don't take yourself too seriously. Learn to laugh at your mistakes. (But don't laugh at yourself when it would be more appropriate to cry.)

Law 4: Investing

Some people call this the principle of seed money, like farmers who put aside ten percent of their crop for seed. In this case it involves giving ten percent of your income after taxes to a worthy cause. The law of investing reinforces the first two principles. Experiment with the ten percent rule and watch the results.

Law 5: Affirming

Put your goals into a positive form. Examples: I will see ten prospects this week; I will eat healthy food and exercise regularly in the upcoming year; I will spend one hour with each of my children every weekend. Express the goal as if it were already true. This strategy provides a positive way to program your mind.

Law 6: Visualizing

A few years ago, a friend of mine had an opportunity to appear on a television quiz show. The grand prize was a week-long cruise for two. In preparation, he made himself a treasure map, cut out a picture of the cruise ship, and wrote beneath it, "I'm now enjoying my cruise." He studied this picture until the day of the quiz show. My friend won ... a portable dishwasher. Two months later, however, he received an offer to audition for a promotional film for a cruise line. He got the part, along with a week's cruise to the Caribbean and a second voyage for two anywhere in the world!

Law 7: Contributing

Remember that you are unique. You have something special to offer your workplace, your family, your community. We all want to feel that we are making a difference. All the successful people I've known felt they were contributing time, talent, and/or money to better their world.

The laws of success can work for you. You need only commit to practicing a new way of thinking, to clearing away the clutter, and to a willingness to risk. You deserve the very best, so find ways to invest something of yourself for the future. Affirm and visualize your goals for success. Share your talent with the world. You and your contributions do make a difference.

■

This is the true joy in life, the being used for a purpose recognized by yourself as a mighty one. The being a force of nature instead of a feverish selfish little clod of ailments and grievances complaining that the world will not devote itself to making you happy.

I am of the opinion that my life belongs to the whole community, and as long as I live it is my privilege to do for it whatever I can.

I want to be thoroughly used up before I die, for the harder I work the more I live. I rejoice in life for its own sake. Life is no brief candle to me. It is a sort of splendid torch which I have got hold of for a moment, and I want to make it burn as brightly as possible before handing it on to future generations.

—George Bernard Shaw

■

■ Beyond Winning and Losing

What is it that stimulates a person to take action—consistent action, aimed at accomplishing a long-term goal? What impels, stimulates, mobilizes, moves a person to excel in anything? Or is the question better phrased in the reverse: What forces, shoves, goads, pressures a person to excel? Is motivation a positively or a negatively driven force?

From what I've seen and experienced, it's both. Different people achieve on the basis of different combinations of forces. There must be an expectation of a positive outcome to accomplish a goal, but people may be driven by a desire to put distance between themselves and failure. Wanting, by itself, doesn't always lead to action. To dream is not to accomplish. Accomplishment takes focused activity: lifting the shovel and digging it into the earth. Imagining alone, no matter how deep the longing, does not produce an outcome.

Where does determination come from? And where does it go when attainment is followed by floundering? I recall Joseph Campbell telling Bill Moyers about a conversation he overheard in which a father was trying to force his son to drink tomato juice. The mother protested, saying her husband shouldn't force the child to do things he doesn't want to do. "He can't go through life doing what he wants to do," the father replied. "If he does only what he wants to do, he'll be dead. Look at me. I've never done a thing I've wanted to do in my life."

Campbell remarked, "That's a man who never followed his bliss. You may have success in life, but then just think of it—what kind of life was it? What good was it—you've never done the thing you wanted to do in all your life. I always tell my students to go where your body and soul want to go. When you have the feeling (of bliss), then stay with it, and don't let anyone throw you off." In Joseph Campbell's eyes, the winner is the one doing and doing and doing and doing that which gives blissful delight—not as an end but as a means. And by doing that which gives enduring pleasure, the doer is at the hub of the roulette wheel, turning and turning in bliss, while others spin on the rim—going up or going down. Says Campbell: "If you are attached to the rim of a wheel of fortune, you will be either above going down, or at the bottom coming up. But if you are at the hub, you are in the same place all the time—centered."

■ The Upcoming Year is Up to "You, Inc."

The singular potential and power of only one goal will boggle your mind. Two possible alternatives exist for your individual achievements for this upcoming year. It can be the greatest, the biggest, and the most exciting year you have ever known. Or it can be a rerun of the same level of achievement and happiness you have known in previous years. Your results for your life depend entirely upon those things which you take command of and make happen. Consequently, You, Inc., is hereby delegated as a committee of one to accept total responsibility for what happens in your life. What would happen this year *if*:

■ You mailed a certified letter each week to only one of your largest-potential-volume prospects at a cost of eighty-five cents over and above the regular postage? Do you think this small investment might prove to be a very important, significant, and intelligent investment in your future?

■ You complimented sincerely an absolute minimum of only one person every day?

■ You asked only one customer each day, "How can I serve you better?"

■ You sent only one letter every day to those customers and prospects on whom you have been too busy to make a personal call?

■ You said gratefully to one person each day, "Thank you. I really appreciate what you did for me"?

■ You smiled only one more time each day than you did each day the previous year?

■ You sought more referrals by inquiring of only one customer each day, "Do you know someone I should be selling to?"

■ You circulated one newsletter each month to all your current and prospective customers?

■ You shared only one new idea a week with your supervisor, client, or a prospect?

■ You spent ninety percent of your time doing things just the same way you did last year, but made whatever adjustments were needed to set aside four hours each week exclusively for pursuing those new accounts or big business increases you want to achieve?

■ You finished reading this list, made a quick mental note of those parts you agreed with, turned the page, and did nothing more?

Nothing can or will happen until You, Inc., takes action. Only when you take action can you create positive changes and have them impact your life. One of the simplest, shortest, most dynamic and beautiful poems ever penned is made up of two-letter words: "If it is to be, it is up to me."

Potential is the cheapest intangible commodity in the world. There's all kinds of potential lying around doing and accomplishing very little or nothing at all. Action has always separated, and always will separate, *potential* from *performance*.

■ Commitment

Commitment is what turns dreams into realities. Your choice is what you want, and your commitment is what allows you to have it. This is the commitment process:

■ You look to see what you want.

■ You choose it.

■ You commit to it.

Commitment makes your choice real. It means: This is going to happen, and I am going to be the one who causes it to happen. Commitment means doing what you say you will do and having what you want, no matter what the obstacles.

You can commit to losing ten pounds, or deciding how to spend a weekend. *What* you commit to is not really important. What matters is the relationship you develop with yourself by committing to what you want.

When you commit, you know you can be counted on to do what you say you will do and to have what you want. For people who have a strong invest-ment in *not* getting what they want, commitment is extremely uncomfortable and oftentimes painful. The painful part is letting go of the attachment to not getting what you want.

Commitment means putting all your resources behind the things you have chosen—putting all your eggs in one basket. It means complete trust in your choice. Commitment means no more holding back, no more waiting to see if something or someone better will come along, no more complaining about obstacles, and no more waiting for someone else to do it for you.

Commitment is not passive, complacent, or hopeful; it is active and deter-mined. Commitment means getting out there and making the thing happen. It means putting one hundred percent of you on the line and going for it. No obsta-cle can stop you when you are committed. When you have chosen someone or something, there is no more confusion or doubt. You have direction, focus, and purpose. Commitment gives you freedom, and it gives you great power. Commitment means that you back yourself and that you stand totally behind your choices. And it means giving yourself access to all the power in your life. In the final analysis, it means being committed to you and your spiritual path.

■ White, Male, Successful: A Sure Brand for a Loser

At first, I didn't recognize him with his stubbly beard, shaggy hair, rumpled clothes, and bloodshot eyes. Then he raised his glass in a weary greeting. Yes, it was George DeSoot, prominent businessman, civic leader, political activist, family man, and all-around swell guy.

"It's me," he said, seeing the look of disbelief on my face. "Come over and buy yourself a drink. I'd buy, but I can no longer afford such extravagant gestures."

I joined him and, as diplomatically as I could, asked what had brought him to such a sorry state. Tell me, what has happened? Did your business falter? Did your happy marriage collapse? Did you develop an incurable slice and suf-fer the shame of a high handicap?

"No, it was much more profound than that. I took a good look at myself and began experiencing guilt, shame, and remorse."

For what?

He choked back a sob and said, "For being white, a male, and successful." Is that all?

"Isn't that enough—that I and those who are like me have brought on almost all of our society's evils and injustices; greedy exploiters; defenders of the status quo; oppressors of everyone who isn't white, male, and successful?"

When did you make this self-analysis?

"It began when my kids came home from college on spring break and told me they had taken a course in political correctness and were ashamed to have a father who was white, male, and successful, and why didn't I go dance with wolves like a decent guy."

Kids—they'll break your heart.

"Then my wife told me she was sick and tired of staying home and making cookies and having teas."

I always thought she made swell cookies.

"And a group of my employees formed a Fairness and Happiness on the Job Study Group and told me that it did not seem fair that I should be rich when they weren't."

But you started and built that company.

"Don't make hollow excuses for me. That is when I looked in the mirror and realized I was a scum."

What did you do?

"Well, I tried to dance with my neighbor's Doberman, but he bit me on the leg, which confirmed my sense of unworthiness. I knew I could not stop being white, since I happened to be born that way. And I could not stop being male (I've always had a terrible fear of surgery, so I ruled that out.) But there was one thing I could change."

And that is?

"Being successful. I realized that was my one major flaw. You seldom hear anyone criticized for being a white male who is a failure. So I rejected my success."

How did you do that?

"I stopped going to my office. I'd sleep late, play Nintendo all afternoon, then come and hang out here until last call."

What happened to your business?

"Went belly up. And the day it happened, I called the employees together and said I was proud to announce that I was no longer rich and asked them to share in my joy before I turned the lights out."

Were they impressed?

"Actually, no. I guess you can't please everybody. Then I went home and told my kids and wife that I was no longer an exploiter and an oppressor."

And they shared in your happiness?

"No, they tried to get me committed, so I grabbed what I could stuff in a suitcase and fled. I've been at peace with myself ever since."

I guess that's what matters the most.

"Yes, so let's drink to the big day that occurred this month."

What day is that?

"April 15. For the first time in my adult life, I didn't have to pay a nickel. I might even write a book."

What will you call it?

"Failure: The Road to Success."

—Mike Royko
©Tribune Media Services Inc.
All rights reserved. Reprinted with permission.

■ "F" Words for Success

In today's society, "F" words are known for their offensiveness, but those that follow, excerpted from a speech by a dear friend Don Landry, can help make our daily lives more meaningful and successful. Don, president of Manor Care Hotel Division, is both a savvy businessperson and an eloquent speaker.

Focused. The ability to zero in on a crystal-clear mission is critical to success. Visualize your goal. Then, visualize yourself in the position of having accomplished the task, having achieved the success. See it. Touch it. Smell it. Feel it. Hear it. Do it often. Your subconscious mind, like a homing pigeon, will guide your actions toward this visualized mission.

Fast. Develop an accurate sense of urgency. Write down your goals along with time frames for accomplishing them.

Flexible. Common sense always overrules procedure. Treating employees equally is unrealistic, but treating employees fairly is critical. Match the talent to the task. Be flexible with job descriptions, but be clear with objectives.

Fresh. Accept the commitment to continuing education as a way of life. Spend your drive time learning rather than punching radio buttons. Invest in cassette tapes on subjects of value to you. Just thirty minutes a day spent with educational audio cassettes adds up to 130 hours a year of continuing education. Also, don't become a "mono-maniac." Develop outside interests, and learn about businesses and industries other than your own.

Fun. Positive thinking works! While you cannot affect things that happen to you on any given day, you can affect the attitude you have toward the things that happen. Focus on the positive. You will be confident, committed, and enthusiastic.

Faith. Yahweh, Christ, Buddah, Mohammed, Allah, atheist, or agnostic—it just doesn't matter. The value of love and kindness is self-evident. All love starts with loving yourself. There is great comfort in being solidly grounded in ethics and integrity. If you do the right thing consistently, you don't even have to consider doing anything else.

Family. You can't hug 'em or kiss 'em or tell 'em that you love them enough—but you should try. Like anything else, you have to work at this. Tell your family what you do and what your job is all about. They care, and will be more understanding when you share your dreams and your fears with them.

Friends. "You can get everything you want by simply helping other people get everything they want," according to Zig Zigler. Use your sales skills to expand and enrich your friendships. Using the "echo" technique, you repeat, with emphasis, the last word or two of someone else's comments.

Fitness. A long-known secret of success is a balanced body, mind, and spirit. You are only going to get one body. Take care of it. Any activity can be groomed into a habit in just twenty-eight days. Get in the habit of exercising twenty minutes a day at least three days a week. Find it difficult? Keep telling yourself the famous Ed Foreman line: "Successful people do what unsuccessful people find hard to do."

Finances. Putting yourself on a firm financial foundation is a step-by-step process. Know the rules. Pay yourself first, then set up the emergency fund and other special accounts. Financial planners can be a great help, but get started now. As John Rhodes put it, "Life by the yard is hard, life by the inch is a cinch."

■ Letting Go of Things

The search for security is often marked by the collecting of things. They seem a fortress against need. We get caught up in the belief that "more is better." Piles of objects often take more time to clean and store than they save. We exhaust ourselves taking care of our property and our social roles.

How many things do you have stored away for the future, like squirrels with their nuts? If you were asked to give away one half, what would you keep? When you dream about fire, what do you rescue from the house? Make a list. Figure out what is weight and what helps you float. Do you know what you want, or just what you've been told to want? Focus on creating and enjoying instead of acquiring and holding on. Build up all of your assets, including health, capacity to love, and appreciation of life. When you let go of the constant urge to acquire, what you truly need begins to flow into your life.

■ The Five Qualities That Make for Success

Integrity. You may seem to succeed for a while without it, but ultimately you will end in failure.

Industry. The industrious person with modest natural equipment gets ahead of the lazy person with superior brains.

Intelligence. Natural intelligence varies greatly from person to person, but it may be sharpened or stunted by one's mental habits.

Knowledge. The man who becomes successful is always learning; he doesn't think of his education as complete when he receives his diploma.

Courage. The type of courage that means taking responsibility and sticking to one's opinion; the type that enables one to fight on despite discouragement; the type that implies integrity, industry, intelligence, and knowledge.

One Is the Only Number

the Neilson ratings came in today
it hasn't been much fun
for all those executive failures
who couldn't stay Number One

Hertz and Avis are at it
vying for very first spot
Mrs. S is depressed by the Best-Dressed List
she didn't stay on top

there's nothing as sad as an old prom queen
staring at the midday sun
thinking about what once had been
when she was Number One

the Wonder of Wall Street died today
his sales were down this year
he died from corporate cancer
which infected him with fear

beware you Wonders of Wall Street
feeling impotent and weak
when the power in your genitals
depends on a winning streak

take heed you overachiever
and Little League mothers too
when you push too far to embody a star
the same might happen to you

One is the winning ticket
that's the American way
One is the Only number
but does it really pay?

—Anonymous

■ Expect the Best

Expecting success is the key to achieving it. When you expect your body to take on a trim, muscular shape, expect a better financial situation, or expect a good performance on the job, you signal your brain to mobilize sensory forces that stimulate the kind of behavior that takes you in your chosen positive direction.

Again, your attitude is instrumental in shaping your reality. Expect the worst and that's what you'll get. To experience the best, you must *believe* the best. You must make positive expectations dominant in your thoughts—short of the point of obsession. You must constantly expect to fulfill the epitome of your desire, the full magnitude of your highest ideal. Nothing less will do.

From this time forward, put the *best* in your mind regarding every aspect of your life: your home life, your job or business situation, your health, your fitness program, your intellectual pursuits, your future. Embrace only the best as you rectify personal problems, as you work toward specific goals, as you plan and perform workouts, as you take on challenging new projects.

This means you must detail—comprehensively and with unerring accuracy—exactly what "best" means to you in each arena of your life. See it, feel it, hear it, nurture it, believe it, and *live* it. This is how you learn to expect the best. This is how you *become* the best.

People who enjoy success have to plan to keep on succeeding. As each goal is achieved, they must look for a new one and keep on scrambling. That's what makes life interesting. When you feel you've got it "made," watch out! It's the first step toward settling back into a pleasant, convenient rut.

One of the tragedies of business is the number of employees, at all levels, who have "mentally" retired. They're resting on their laurels, just along for the ride. They aren't looking for new challenges and aren't interested in ways of doing things differently or better; they're no longer much concerned about the competition or the customer. Like anyone who coasts, there's only one place for them to go—downhill. Keep alive, keep challenging yourself until the day you quit. When growth stops, decay begins.

Most people who obtain success have learned to forget past failure and concentrate on the present. Babe Ruth was once asked what he thought about when he struck out. "I think about hitting home runs," the Babe answered. When the average person strikes out, he or she feels hurt and ashamed and dwells on the failure. Yet, as Teddy Roosevelt said, "Show me a man who makes no mistakes, and I'll show you a man who doesn't do things." Failure is the first step to success. Do the best with what you've got, and do it expecting to achieve the best.

■ Self-Discipline: The Master Key to Success

On the long, hard road to success, one characteristic alone will determine whether you ever reach your goal. It is not intelligence. It is not talent. It is not luck. It is not "who you know."

Without self-discipline, all the brains, inspiration, and education in the world won't get you past the starting gate of achievement and self-fulfillment. With it, there is truly no goal that's out of reach, because self-discipline keeps you on the path to success, no matter how long it takes or what obstacles may be thrown in your way.

In our "quick fix" society, many people think self-discipline means suffering and self-denial. Yet nothing could be further from the truth.

Self-discipline is what enables you to achieve lifelong gratification—through the rewards that come from the patient planning and realization of your most cherished goals. Though many people seem born with an iron will, self-discipline is not an inherited trait. It can be systematically learned and systematically applied.

Isn't it time to light a fire of persistence inside you that will not go out until you've succeeded in your most important endeavors? You'll see what a difference it makes in achieving your goals when you are truly in control of your life.

■ Become a Decision-Maker

The difference between success and failure in life can often be measured in seconds ... the seconds it takes to make a decision. Decision-making has been called the most prized quality in successful executives. This same ability also is an absolute necessity for all who wish to excel in the field of sales and climb the financial ladder to the top.

Decisions come in two forms—the instant variety and the incubating type. The first type involves great money-making ideas that come to you in a flash, while the second is based on facts that have been gathered from many sources. In either case, we think we have a problem making a decision, but the truth is making no decision is also making a decision. It's a decision not to act.

What you tell yourself in the first few seconds following an idea will many times determine your height on the success ladder. Generally speaking, decisions to act are far more valuable and constructive than decisions to wait—to procrastinate.

A recent questionnaire filled out by more than 25,000 unsuccessful men and women in the business field showed that lack of decision-making skills was close to the top of the list of the thirty major causes for failure. Since the twin of no-decision is procrastination, let's look at some of the factors inherent in both. The jealousy, negativism, and ignorance of friends, relatives, and co-workers can be a contributing factor. Experts recommend that we keep our ideas secret, sharing them only with those from whom we are assured a positive response and feedback. Your peer group will seldom want to see you advance beyond them, so they are likely to find fault with your ideas.

Thomas Edison said that seventy-five percent of all ideas would work except for the lack of persistence in those generating them. Persistence defeats procrastination and helps develop self-confidence. Here's a good way to help you make decisions you will not regret. First define your idea on paper. Draw a line down the center and mark the two columns "pro" and "con." List the number of good reasons for going ahead with your decision under the "pro" column. List the minuses. Then add up your scores. If you have more gos than nos ... plan ahead and decide to get started.

■ Are You a Success Slob?

Do you:

- Talk about yesterday's triumphs and friendships?
- Not enjoy the action of today?
- Tend to be unhappy with yourself and others?
- Resent the legitimate success and happiness of others?
- Get greedy in relationships with others and want that extra share that makes further contacts difficult or impossible?
- Need endless reassurance or guarantees from others?
- Keep actively working on projects and keep material around from activities that have long ceased to be of any importance or value?

If these success-slob traits sound familiar to you, it's time to be ruthless with your past. The great swimmer Mark Spitz acquired an impressive collection of medals after his phenomenal success. But he did not swim future races with gold metals around his neck. Don't drown yourself with your past.

■ The Winning Attitude

Experts tell us that attitude is a key factor in personal improvement. Attitude relates to the desire to learn and progress and the persistence that conquers lethargy and overcomes obstacles. These traits are motivated by willpower. Do you have winning attitudes? Here are some things to check:

Realistic viewpoint. The realistic way of looking at things doesn't mean surrendering to circumstances or drifting instead of driving. It implies understanding what can be done, and how, and whether the goal justifies what it takes to reach it ... no brooding over past mistakes or needless fears about the future.

Methodical pacing. Experienced mountain climbing guides set a deliberate pace. They seem to plod along, never hurrying, taking advantage of every means of avoiding extra exertion. Yet they reach objectives sooner and with less evidence of fatigue than tenderfeet who move more impulsively.

Alibis and excuses. An Englishman was asked why British soldiers had a reputation for bravery. He replied, "I don't think our troops are any braver than those of other nations—they just stay that way a little longer." Even successful salesmen have doubts, worries, financial setbacks, and other shortcomings. But rather than becoming discouraged by these normal hazards, they show faith in themselves and keep pushing ahead.

Confident image. Until Roger Bannister broke the record in the mile many years ago, it was thought that four minutes was an insurmountable barrier. Since he showed it could be done, the mile has repeatedly been run in under four minutes.

■ Bring It to the Rainbow

It takes a shade more effort, a bit more time, but once you've mastered the art, life is never quite the same. Albert Rogerts is an indefatigable shoeshine boy at a New York hotel, and his rhythmic artistry with polish and brush leaves a shine that almost hurts your eyes. I once asked him if he ever got tired. Albert replied that he didn't because he wasn't just shining shoes.

This shoeshine artist has something in common with Will Edgers, a Vermont farmer who sells firewood. Some friends ordered half a cord last fall while we were visiting them. Will didn't just dump the wood from his truck. He made a small platform of stones, and then carefully stacked the wood at a slant to keep rain water from standing on the pile. When he surveyed his handiwork, Will said quietly, "Wood's a pretty thing, now ain't it? Growin', split, or burnin'."

Albert and Will, each in his own way, have discovered a compelling secret that makes everything they do pay off in terms of greater satisfaction, deeper self-realization. Pablo Casals, the world-famous cellist, put it into words while giving a lesson to a young student. She played the notes just as they were written. Casals played the same notes, but they throbbed and glowed. He asked the girl to repeat the passage several times, each time demonstrating the special quality he wanted her to bring to it. Casals' advice: Bring it to the rainbow—always the rainbow. When the pupil finally did, her face lit up in pure joy.

The rainbow is the glow that crowns the all-out effort to do a job, any kind of job, as well as you possibly can. It takes a shade more effort, a bit more time, but once you have experienced the mixture of elation, pride, and relief that comes from creating rainbows, life is never quite the same.

You can say with honesty: This is good; it has a part of me in it. Then all tasks that once seemed boring and routine become meaningful and rewarding.

May I suggest some simple rules for bringing rainbows to your own work and life?

Give it everything you've got. "The champion isn't necessarily the person who has the most," Dr. Laurence E. Morehouse of UCLA's Human Performance Laboratories told me. "But the blue-ribbon winner is always the person who gives the most. The champion is willing to risk all on the task. The runner-up, who may have equal or superior potential, holds something back."

Often it's the fear of failure that prevents us from going all out. It's as if we were preparing to excuse failure in advance, so we can say we weren't really trying. Paradoxically, losing oneself in the task at hand is the only way to find oneself. The more you give, the more you have to give—and the more rainbows you create.

Give it one more try. To get material for a book, *How to Study Better,* Professor Eugene Ehrlich from Columbia University interviewed hundreds of students. Some had barely passing grades, others were average students, some had all A's. Dr. Ehrlich reported that there wasn't much difference in their native intelligence. "The one thing that distinguished the A student was the 'baker's dozen complex.' After hitting the books as hard as they could, most students figured that was that. The A student, however, gave it one more try for good measure."

It's hard to experience repeated failure and still go on trying. But sometimes it's even harder to go on after achieving limited success. It's tempting to say that a pretty good job will do, but Gustave Flaubert rewrote his great novel, *Madame*

Bovary, at least three times. He was still so dissatisfied that he considered burning the manuscript. Flaubert gave it one last try—and the result was a classic.

Take a proprietary attitude toward your job. The electrical wizard Charles Steinmetz used to work in his laboratory at General Electric for hours after the staff had gone home. A colleague asked him one day why he did it. He was curious because Steinmetz didn't have to prove anything—he got the same salary no matter how many hours he worked. Steinmetz looked up from his workbench and told his friend, "It doesn't matter how much you get or who pays you. You are always working for yourself."

Tackle little jobs as if they were big ones. Some people don't think their jobs are worth their best efforts. They are always saving themselves for the big break ... which never comes. They don't realize that the big job consists of many little jobs, all of which have to be done well.

I know a Navajo silversmith in Tucson who goes right on creating fine jewelry while most of his competitors have compromised on workmanship and materials by making gewgaws for the tourist trade. One day I asked him why he spent so much time turning out little pieces of art when he could cash in so easily with inferior workmanship. "I tried making junk," he said. "It was like making false money. It fooled other people, but it didn't fool me. I look at my bankbook maybe once or twice a month. But I have to live with myself every day."

Doing something we can call our own satisfies a deep need in us. The material world in which we live is stubborn and chaotic. All of us feel the urge to impose our order on some small part of it. This is the only way we discover who we are. It is the way we create rainbows.

■

Pearls of Wisdom

Do the thing and you will have the power.
—*Ralph Waldo Emerson*

■

A man's best things are nearest to him, lie close about his feet.
—*Richard Monkton Milnes*

■

■

*It is when we try to make our will conform to God's will that
we begin to use it rightly.*
—Bill W.

■

A single arrow is easily broken, but not ten in a bundle.
—Japanese proverb

■

*All things are possible until they are proved impossible—and
even the impossible may only be as of now.*
—Pearl S. Buck

■

*Things turn out best for the people who make the best out of
the way things turn out.*
—Art Linkletter

■

Until you try, you don't know what you can't do.
—Henry James

■

*I have always known that at last I would take this road,
but yesterday I did not know that it would be today.*
—Narihira (translated by Kenneth Rexroth)

■

*He who knows others is wise. He who knows himself
is enlightened.*
—Lao-tzu

■

■

Having your dreams fulfilled can be more therapeutic than having them analyzed.
—Tom Feltenstein

■

A great deal of talent is lost to the world for the want of a little courage.
Every day sends to their grave obscure men whom timidity prevented from making a first effort.
—Sydney Smith

■

Every now and then I think about my own death, and I think about my own funeral ... I don't want a long funeral. And if you get somebody to deliver the eulogy, tell them not to talk too long ... Tell them not to mention that I have a Nobel Peace Prize ... Tell them not to mention that I have three hundred or four hundred other awards ... I'd like someone to mention that day, that Martin Luther King, Jr., tried to give his life to serving others. I'd like for somebody to say that day that Martin Luther King, Jr., tried to love someone....

Say that I was a drum major for justice. Say that I was a drum major for peace. That I was a drum major for righteousness. And all of the other shallow things will not matter. I won't have fine and luxurious things of life to leave behind. But I just want to leave a committed life behind.

—Martin Luther King, Jr.
Ebenezer Baptist Church, Atlanta
February 4, 1968

■

■ Personal Truths of Sam Walton, Creator of Walmart Stores

■ Commit to your business. I think I overcame every single one of my personal shortcomings by the sheer passion I brought to my work.

■ Share your profits with all of your associates and treat them as partners. In turn, they will treat you as a partner, and together you will perform beyond your wildest expectations.

■ Communicate everything you possibly can to your partners. The more they know, the more they'll understand. Information is power, and the gain you get from empowering your associates more than offsets the risk of informing your competitors.

Ethical Cornerstones

—

Kindness in words creates confidence,
Kindness in thinking creates profoundness,
Kindness in giving creates love.

—Lao-Tzu

CHAPTER 3

Lately, I've done a lot of thinking about ethics in business. One of my major responsibilities is getting new clients for my company, a medium-sized marketing and franchising consulting practice. Trying to win new business has to be one of the most intense forms of business competition. Every pitch is a battle of ideas and personality. I face ethical situations every day that would tempt a saint. And, quite frankly, I'm unhappy with the level of ethics in today's business world in general—not because I have all the answers, but because I don't see many people even thinking about the questions.

It's been my experience that when there are discussions of corporate ethics, they often center on topics like product safety, the environment, or employee rights. But while these subjects are certainly important, they seem to have little to do with the scandals that have plagued our society over the last few years: insider trading, influence peddling by former top political appointees, television evangelists ripping off their congregations, collusion among military contractors, and outright bribery at the Pentagon ... just to mention a few.

To my way of thinking, there are four simple principles that can be used to analyze and resolve the ethical dilemmas that often characterize business competition. Sometimes these principles are in conflict with each other, but I think most people in business will agree that they can be used as a practical guide to the ethics of business competition.

First, there is full disclosure. Anything that can be completely disclosed without embarrassment is inherently ethical. I know of no exception to this rule. The reverse is not necessarily true, however. Business competition involves secrecy and surprise, but something that must be kept a secret is not necessarily unethical. An inherent part of the competitive process is to try to learn or surmise your competitor's plans and to deceive him or her with regard to your own.

Second, there is aiding and abetting—promoting or profiting from the unethical act of someone else, which is itself unethical. I've occasionally been approached by someone who promises to recommend my firm, provided we agree to pay a finder's fee if we get the business. Paying a finder's fee to secure business is not unethical in itself. But if I have reason to suspect that the recipient is deceiving his principal, I am just as guilty as he is.

Third, we all have fiduciary responsibilities. It is unethical to betray the trust of those whose interests we are being paid to represent. This includes our employer, our stockholders, our employees, our clients, and, for a Pentagon employee or military contractor, it includes the taxpayer. In any personal service business, such as marketing, this can be a complex issue.

Recently, the entire top echelon of a fine New York ad agency resigned to start a new competitive company. Something similar happened a few months ago to the mergers and acquisitions department of a leading investment banking firm. Obviously, we should all be free to work for whomever we wish, and taking the risk of starting a business from scratch is a commendable entrepreneurial activity. But if I plan my own venture while I am still employed and paid by someone who trusts me to be acting in his or her interest, and if my new business is designed to take clients away from my employer, how commendable, and how risky, is that?

Fiduciary responsibilities are also the second edge of the double-edged ethical sword. If I choose not to pursue a casino account, for instance, because it would violate my own personal ethical standards, I ought to balance that decision against the economic interests of my employees or the success of my company. But there are usually two sides to such issues—such as doing business with firms in South Africa or working for companies that promote gambling and sell cigarettes. Discussing these issues with any employer in advance of having to make decisions about them would help immensely.

Fourth, and finally, there is what I call the level-playing-field rule. Anyone who believes in and profits from the free-market system is honor-bound not to undermine it. This rule covers a wide territory. No collusion with your competitors, for instance, and no denying economic opportunities to others for reasons such as race, gender, or religion. Most companies and most businesspeople are committed, at least philosophically, to the belief that a free-market system is beneficial to us all. So it would be an act of sheer hypocrisy to deny someone access to this economic system for reasons of sex or color.

Ethics, in my opinion, should be taught in business school. Children should learn moral values from their parents and teachers. But no, it is not too late to raise a businessperson's ethical standards just because he or she is now an adult. Adults really are capable of improving themselves. That's what capitalism is all about—people having the freedom to better themselves economically without hindrance, by choosing their own work and making money from their own efforts. It is every boss's responsibility to himself or herself, to his or her company, and to society as a whole, to ensure that his or her people at least think about the ethical consequences of their business activities from time to time.

Make money. Have fun. Be ethical. These are the three keys to a successful business career. They were given to me years ago when I first took a job with a very large hamburger chain headquartered in Chicago. I've never forgotten them, and I've repeated them quite often over the years. Sometimes an eyebrow will go up. Ethics? Some people don't think of that as a necessary part of a first-day briefing. It's not in their frame of reference. And that's exactly what the problem is.

In spite of my casual management style and one-on-one way of doing business, I take the way I do business, my "ethical cornerstones," very seriously. Let me share with you my sense of management style and the way I like to do business with my clients.

Date

Name
Company
Address
City, State, Zip Code

Dear Client:

As promised, I'd like to share with you the style and character of Tom Feltenstein.

Several years ago, either consciously or unconsciously, I made a very basic decision ... not to run a common business. That is, once I had the opportunity to be in business for myself, I exercised my right to be different. The question has always been, was I up to the task? I always sought opportunity rather than security; I have been willing to take the calculated risk—to dream and to build, to fail and to succeed. I am trying to build my company with people who prefer the challenges of a growing business to a guaranteed existence in a lackluster organization. They are people who are looking for the thrill of fulfillment rather than trying to maintain the status quo. I want to be able to look myself, my clients, my peers, my partners, and my detractors in the eye and say, "Let the record speak for itself."

Let me spend the next several minutes talking about Tom Feltenstein's style—personal and business—just in case I haven't been able to articulate it fully during our meetings.

Historically, I've had a style that has been different from others'. I've never been fortunate enough to have "a place in the sun" handed to me.

I've had to do it the hard way. I've had to develop my *own* style. And in the process of hand-forging that style, I've gained something else—my style and set of beliefs have taken strong, deep root and have become the basis of my character.

Please bear with me. I want very much to let you inside me so you'll know exactly how I think and how potent our business relationship and friendship can be ... and is. Much of what I publish in my monthly newsletter ("Personal Communique") expresses part of who I am today. Such messages as, "People want to know how much you care, before they care how much you know," and, "Today!" are simple sayings that quickly convey my "do it now" philosophy. Here are some expressions of belief which describe my style:

The first and most important cornerstone is the way I approach solving clients' problems. You can call it enthusiasm, energy, or intensity—but those are just ordinary words. My style is digging, fighting, and scratching. Energy is the positive force. Complacency doesn't exist. I've always said that there is no ceiling on effort, that hard work never hurt anybody.

My style is punctuated with a competitive fire that can be characterized as overkill. To me, overkill results in dissatisfaction with merely doing what's okay. Overkill means detesting that part of me which says, "It's okay." Overkill demands that I ask these questions: What else should I do? What else can I do? How can I build a better marketing plan?

In some situations, overkill doesn't mean intensity and working hard so much as it means a willingness to work *harder* at the dirtier, less glamorous parts of our business. It means that any job worth doing is worth doing well.

Having a sense of urgency, a sense of doing it now, doing it today, is part of my style. Overkill drives me to do my job faster and better than anyone else—or at the very least, to bust my butt trying. Overkill is one cornerstone of my style.

The second part of my style has to do with openness, candor, and truth. I'm committed to full disclosure to you on everything I do. I would hope you would be the same with me. Full disclosure is disarming. Early on in my career, a man I was dealing with said, "I've got you figured out: You use the honesty bit." He was right—and with good reason. Openness and candor are a vital part of integrity.

Telling the truth is a matter of ethics. That's why I have gone to great lengths to communicate to you everything I'd like to see happen, to share with you the execution of the game plan. I'm out there trying very hard to earn my wings every day.

This third broad point about my style has to do with ego. I take my business very seriously, but try not to take myself too seriously. Business is hard enough on its own without throwing in the additional difficulty of an uncontrolled ego. People who have been around me for any length of time know that my tolerance for the negative is very short. My blood pressure goes off the charts at garden variety complaining—when someone wants to feed his or her own fragile ego by telling you what's wrong with others. Discussing what's wrong in the context of a solution is terrific! Using dissatisfaction with something negative to create a positive is a wonderful and, in fact, a beautiful process.

But if you aren't willing to make yourself and your ideas part of the solution, then I believe you've added to and have become part of the problem. People with strong, controlled egos—those who are willing to take the risk and responsibility for fixing a problem, and who don't need to build their egos by trading on the problem—are, in my opinion, the real strength of any organization.

My fourth point has to do with human dealings. I believe in courtesy, in saying thank you to show appreciation. I want our company to be known as a basic, down-to-earth, get-it-done company. I have put a great deal of emphasis on establishing a comfort zone with you—where mutual respect and understanding have allowed for lines of resistance to melt and a real relationship to form. It can only grow from here.

I'm emotional about my relationships. When a shared experience expands the comfort zone, the business can really be fun. Work, yes, but also with a shared dream that generates a real thrust in building a business together. No exhilaration compares with overcoming a challenge with friends. If there is a problem, let's fix it ... together.

My fifth and last point has to do with management style. It takes a strong will to manage well. Our management styles may be different, but that doesn't mean we have to be isolated. Quite the contrary. I manage by example. I believe success in our company is born of doing what we say. My style, as I believe yours to be, is to be willing to ask for extraordinary commitment and work performance.

Crap rolls uphill in my business. The higher you go, the more problems you deal with. Top people make more money ... for their resiliency, for their ability to keep others going after setbacks, and for keeping the momentum strong after victories.

I continually remind our staff, and myself, of the importance of the business we have. It's a message we can never spend too much time conveying in words and actions. As exciting and heady as a major new business win is, we must deliver to our current business everything we promise in new business, and then some. I promise you this: You will get everything we promise ... and more. You can count on it.

All my best,

Tom Feltenstein

■ Ethics Check

The following ten questions cover the qualities of integrity, strength of character, honesty, fairness, and courage, which constitute the ingredients of ethical behavior. Answer the questions as honestly as you can, giving yourself a score of 1 (for "always or very frequently") through 10 (for "never") for each.

1. How often have you failed to keep a promise you made to a colleague, a subordinate, a superior, a customer, a friend, or your partner?

2. How often do you keep your opinion to yourself when you know it's not the one shared by your superiors, colleagues, or mate?

3. How often do you behave one way with your superiors (mild, respectful, considerate, pleasant) and another way with your subordinates (rough, abrupt, unsmiling, inconsiderate)?

4. A certain act is not illegal, but seems morally questionable to you. How often do you do it anyway?

5. If doing business requires you to go against your own values, how often do you do so anyway?

6. How often do you take what you're not entitled to—property or time from your employer or friends, money or valuables you find, etc.?

7. How often do you misrepresent the facts, distort the truth, or simply say or imply things you know to be untrue in order to achieve your business objectives or interests?

8. If you find out that a practice that's wrong, unfair, or unethical is taking place, how often do you do nothing about it?

9. If a colleague is clearly subjected to inhumane or grossly unfair treatment or abuse, how often do you ignore it and just mind your own business?

10. If dealing with others fairly yields a certain level of return, while dealing with others unfairly yields a much higher return, how often do you choose the latter?

The scoring methodology takes into consideration the fact that we are all human, and probably nobody behaves in a one hundred percent manner one hundred percent of the time. How do you score?

-

Accountability

Accountability is the opportunity to live with choice rather than accidentally. Accountability is the opportunity to carve out the future rather than sit back and have it happen to you. Transformation lives in accountability. Without accountability, with mere promises and declarations, there is no transformation; there is, at best, peak performance.

A promise has real power. A promise made from the stand that who you are is your word engages you as a participant. You cease to be a spectator, and words become actions that actually impact the world. With a promise you create a condition that supports your commitment rather than your moods. When motivational dialogue comes up about your preference versus your commitments, and you disregard the dialogue in favor of doing what you said you would do solely because you said so, you distinguish yourself from your psychology. In that moment you are your word as an action, rather than only as an idea you have.

In that moment, the promise becomes who you are rather than something you said—and your relationship to the world shifts. You find yourself producing results that seem discontinuous and unpredictable from the point of view of the spectator. The experience is one of joy, fearlessness, irrepressible energy, and satisfaction. Transformation exists, not only when we speak about it, but when we empower others to speak it. The success of our work will be measured by our ability to penetrate the prevailing conceptual reality with the possibility that transformation is.

—Werner Erhard

-

■ The Games People Play

A few months ago, I was invited to dine at the offices of an executive I had known off and on for many years. The luncheon was served in an elegant room next to the executive's office. It was an inordinately formal four-course affair, served by a chef attired in a white jacket who would enter with each new course from a hidden door. The conversation was intriguing. The meal was splendid. The whole experience seemed choreographed to soothe guests and impress them.

I know that I was impressed—not only by the executive's hospitality, but by the fact that he seemed to have a full-time kitchen at his disposal. He had come a long way since I first knew him. At the end of the meal, as the chef refilled our cups of coffee, the host reinforced the impression. He praised the chef on the richness of the meal, patted his stomach, and joyfully added, "I'm glad I'm not eating here this evening." A nice touch, I thought. He had made sure I knew he had a chef on staff day and night.

I later learned that the meal was, in fact, brought in by a catering service and that the chef worked for the caterer. But that didn't diminish my appreciation of his effort. I was particularly impressed by how artfully he had played with the truth to suggest the chef was on staff. He hadn't said anything that was an outright lie. He didn't have to. He had simply timed his remarks and omitted certain facts to achieve the desired effect. It was more a sin of omission than of commission.

This little episode is just one of the many games people play with the truth each day. I don't necessarily endorse this man's verbal sleight of hand. But it's hard to condemn it, because all of us play such games dozens of times each day. We usually don't have any other choice.

Let's say a friend has just received a bad haircut and asks you, "How do I look?" How would you respond? Most people would fib or use a euphemism that gets them off the hook. Instinct tells them there's no reward for telling the truth. All you'll do is hurt a friend. The fact is, complete honesty is a perpetual risk-reward decision. What do you gain by telling the truth, and what do you stand to lose if you shade it a little bit in your favor?

Even the most saintly and scrupulous among us play the game. For example, most people who find twenty-five cents on the floor of a movie theater would put it in their pocket because the effort of returning it is not worth twenty-five cents, nor is there any risk or reward in doing so. No one will be grateful for the rescue of a quarter, and no one will think ill of you for keeping it.

However, if you found $25,000 on the floor, you still might pocket it, but you'd think about returning it or locating the rightful owner. The rewards and risks are much greater. Someone will be grateful if you do the right thing. And a lot of people might regard it as inexcusable if you don't.

Most people play games with the truth in order to conceal an error or a failure to do something. If they're late for a meeting or miss a deadline or need to cancel lunch with a friend, they'll make up an excuse that isn't likely to be challenged.

People also tend to fiddle with the truth when they are dealing with a computer. I see this all the time with business travel. A harried executive needs to make a particular flight but forgot to make a reservation. He has two options. He can rush up to the ticket counter, admit that he doesn't have a reservation, and place himself at the ticket agent's mercy. Or he can blame the computer: "I made a reservation," he can say. "It was confirmed." The risk is minimal. The reward is tangible: Blaming the computer makes the agent try a little harder to get him on that flight. If the flight is really important, a lot of people might stretch the truth to make it.

The telephone probably generates the most white lies in business— because you can say virtually anything and the person on the other end of the line has no visual evidence to disprove you. If I think the timing is not to my advantage to take someone's call, I will instruct my secretary, "Tell him I'm on an overseas call. I'll get back to him." (I do call back when the time is right for me.) That excuse sounds better than telling him I haven't got the time or that I'm doing something that's more important than taking his call.

Sometimes playing with the truth can make you look good. For example, recreational tennis is a sport where, if you let it, every line call can become a struggle with the truth. The obvious solution is to call the lines exactly as you see them. But it's tricky. Which way do you go when you think the ball might be out, but you didn't see it clearly? It depends on what's at stake. If winning at all costs is crucial to you, you might call it in your favor—and damn the impression it makes.

On the other hand, if your opponent is a potential customer and you are trying to impress him with your fairness, you might give him the benefit of the doubt. You might legitimately say, "I didn't see it, but it was probably in." Do this consistently on the close calls and you can soar in your opponent's estimation. He'll not only like you, he'll want to do business with you because he can rely on you to give the close calls in business to him.

■

Live Consciously

If we can be courageous one more time than we are fearful, trusting one more time than anxious, cooperative one more time than we are competitive, forgiving one more time than we are vindictive, loving one more time than we are hateful, we will have moved closer to the next breakthrough in our evolution. One warning: Evolutionary behavior is addictive. Once you start, it's very hard to stop. After all, why live and evolve unconsciously when we can live consciously and, at the same time, speed up the process of evolution for ourselves and others?

—*Jonas Salk*

■

■ The Elusive Nature of Integrity

In the operating room of a great hospital, a young nurse had her first day of full responsibility. "You've removed eleven sponges, doctor," she said to the surgeon. "We used twelve."

"I removed them all," the doctor assured her. "We'll close the incision now."

"No," the nurse objected, "we used twelve."

"I'll take the responsibility," the surgeon told her.

"You can't do that," she said. "Think of the patient."

The doctor smiled, lifted his foot, and showed the nurse the missing sponge. "You'll do," he said.

He had been testing her for integrity—and she had it.

This story, told by noted editor and author Arthur Gordon, illustrates a key component of integrity: having the courage of your convictions, doing what you believe is right, and not fearing to speak out. Integrity is sorely needed today, when we seem to be more interested in looking good, making a good showing, and receiving favorable press coverage. At the root of our existence is a need for the reemergence of integrity as a common element in the collective character of humankind.

This elusive quality cannot be self-proclaimed but only observed in others. Most acts of integrity are performed in private—not subject to public view. Those who have integrity have discovered something that the rest of the world must learn: that integrity, which many look upon as being composed of sacrifice, struggle, and nonadvantageous decision-making, actually makes life easier, joyful, and powerful.

Here's an example. After the fall youth soccer season was over, the head coach of the second-grade team resigned. The assistant coach took over before the spring season to ensure continuity for his young players. Less than a month before the first game, the new coach changed jobs to a high-powered executive position requiring long hours and travel. His dilemma was the conflict between the demands of the new job and the needs of the soccer team. The coach decided to honor his commitment to the players and their parents.

He was rewarded for toughing it out. His team, playing in a more difficult division, had a good season. But the best part of the story is what happened on the job, where he rose to the demands and earned a bonus for his outstanding performance.

America and the world have been waiting for a return to integrity. We began a cycle with the social revolution of the sixties, the self-exploration of the seventies, and the high-tech disenfranchising of the eighties. The cycle is about to come full circle in the nineties with the return of the exploration of and return to human values. Recapturing the spirit and essence of integrity is the crucial link to our ability to make the future work.

We tend to have some curious reactions to integrity. For example, we discount acts of integrity by others, not believing that they did something simply because they thought it was the right thing. And we are quick to condemn others who lack integrity while overlooking our own lapses. Integrity is really many things. It has many synonyms, none of which is sufficient: trustworthiness, loyalty, virtue, sincerity, candor, uprightness, honesty. Perhaps it is the pivotal concept of what it means to be human, and it certainly involves accepting one's humanity. Integrity is also the avoidance of deception and expediency. It is being complete and undivided, being the same person to everyone. It's not noble, not altruistic. Rather, it is a practical vehicle for living effectively. It is maintaining values steadfastly and focusing on what you believe is right.

Who has integrity? The immediate answer is those who demonstrate the quality and keep making the higher choice. It is an active, living virtue that must be displayed again and again to remain intact. It is not something to be mastered and put on the shelf. Those who have integrity have it now. The characteristic can't be saved and stored, although certainly its practice increases the likelihood of recurrence. Perhaps integrity is an ingrained habit nurtured in family or small town settings apart from the mobile, transient, frenzied pace of contemporary society. Maybe it is found only where stroking and support systems exist.

For all but a few of us, integrity is a long time in the making. If where we draw the line determines our integrity, how do we determine where to draw it? We may want to study the internal reward system used by those with a high degree of integrity, and then adopt that system in our own lives.

In today's environment, the scales often tip the other way. Displays of integrity may be subject to ridicule. The need to toe the line of corporate culture can lure the individual away from what he or she knows is right. We have a diminishing number of role models. A lifetime of integrity can be lost in a dash. The tensions of the moment or the focus on material rewards can leave the concept on shaky ground. And it seems that there are fewer and fewer penalties for not having integrity.

Perhaps that is the heart of the matter. Integrity is missing in society when the notion of "you versus me" prevails. The obsession with success and the predominance of the materialistic images of Madison Avenue and Hollywood that are invading our living rooms usher in a contagious downward cycle.

Americans today thirst for quick approval, scramble for positioning, and yearn for an appearance of security. Some causes: more of us living in urban and suburban settings, and fierce competition among baby boomers for jobs, housing, and mates. The price: The trappings of getting ahead become more important than homage to lofty virtue. Integrity is missing when large numbers of individuals are isolated and disenfranchised from the mainstream, when concern about how to get from A to B conveniently replaces how to serve humanity, how to contribute to society.

Innocent children often have some ingrained notion of integrity, only to lose most of it when they reach adulthood. What happened? Some lose integrity by believing their dedication must be ideal or total. When they recognize that they can't live up to such high standards, they rationalize and give up. Other times, the loss of integrity begins with not believing in the oneness of humanity. Such notions as "no one will know, why bother?" or "just this one time" are cracks in the leaky dike.

I believe we can instinctively identify people who are devoid of integrity. The trait is absent when we focus on tangible losses instead of internal gains. One loses integrity by giving in to social pressure, moving to a less supportive environment, blaming outside factors, and simply not noticing that integrity is slipping away.

A life of integrity is a goal or ideal to aim for, but there will always be lapses. A snowball of frustration can occur after just one slip. The notion that no one will know about the car we nicked in the parking lot insulates us from dealing with the real issue and our responsibilities as human beings. Improving our integrity means pursuing the truth wherever and whenever we find it, standing our ground even if no one else follows. It means not accepting the status quo, avoiding the small lie, not repeating rumors. Speaking about integrity, studying the lessons of history, and simply deciding to improve will all help. The quest to improve integrity means giving anonymously, making and keeping commitments, accepting responsibility, and continually looking for situations to practice our growing awareness. Improvement means making the call we have been avoiding, striving for fidelity in relationships, and associating with others who display this elusive quality on a regular basis.

Many people don't understand the benefits of honing integrity because they believe that the act involves blood, sweat, and tears. To the contrary, those with high levels of integrity achieve superior physical and emotional well-being. The trait we strive for gives meaning and purpose to life and conveys enduring values that transcend contemporary fads and follies. It allows for boldness and decisive action, and helps eliminate self-doubt and muted self-expression.

There are still other benefits to the quest. Raising children in the spirit of integrity helps them function adequately in society. Practicing it in our profession leads to prosperity, because customers return to the store or the person who gave them a fair deal. The display of integrity by one individual can inspire others around him or her. Integrity inspires trust, respect, and peace of mind in others. The integrity of those with big dreams enables others to latch on to the vision. In fact, integrity creates a context in which all things are possible. Wouldn't it be magnificent if people were to act with integrity just one more time each day? Even a modest increase will transform society.

■ The Practicality of Integrity

"Phonies finish last." Do you agree with that statement? According to a recent survey by the American Management Association, most American business-es do. They placed integrity at the top of their priority list for important commodities and values in the workplace. You may be saying to yourself that integrity is a good idea but it's not practical.

Think again. Higher sales, greater earnings, and stronger relationships are as much a part of integrity as quality, completeness, and soundness. Why? Because people are loyal to products, services, and people they can trust. Consider these questions and you'll see why integrity pays off:

Would you make a major decision to buy from a person you didn't trust?

Would you give a person your full loyalty if he or she demonstrated shaky integrity?

Would you continue to buy products or services from someone who consistently supplied second-rate service and follow-through?

As noted psychologist Dr. Harry Link states, "Principles, and people of principle, are the life blood of democracy and not something to be sneered at, as has become fashionable in our time." Principles are the life blood of selling, as well. The strength of an individual and his company is directly related to their reputations, and good reputations are based on integrity.

■ The Many Forms of Candor

I think a lot of businesspeople have a problem with candor. Perhaps that's because so many of us put a premium on secrecy and finesse in business. In a sales situation, we tend to highlight our product or service's virtues rather than its liabilities. In a negotiation, we take pride in being able to disclose information when it's to our advantage rather than the other side's. In managing people, we prefer to give them only as much information as we feel they need. In other words, we make a virtue of our ability to obscure a situation.

Of course, that's not bad at all. We all face situations when being less than candid is the most prudent form of action (and inflicts no damage to our conscience and ethical well-being).

A car salesman, for example, is not necessarily obliged to tell a customer that the model he admires in the showroom is rated fourth in its class in gas mileage. That's not candor; it's bad salesmanship. Why steer customers to the competition?

More Virtues in Telling More

But all this emphasis on being less than candid perhaps blinds us to the considerable virtues of candor itself. Candor comes in many guises. The most common, of course, is the crude, blunt variety. You tell people what you're thinking and hope they appreciate your honesty. When in doubt, I am a very frontal person. If I have done something wrong, I admit it. If I am mad, I say so. If I am disappointed, I let people know it. This sort of candor is not only good therapy, but I notice that it has a cleansing effect on some of the messiest situations. Sunshine, as they say, is the best disinfectant.

When You're Wrong

The best time to employ this sort of candor is when you have made a mistake. People generally have two options when they are in a jam. They can try to obscure the situation, or they can open their soul and tell the truth. Candor is a better option. If you can be candid with people in those moments when you have achieved far less than your best, you'll find that they are more likely: (a) to remember your candor instead of your trespasses, (b) to forgive you, and (c) to be equally candid with you.

Underpromise the Competition

Candor is spectacularly valuable when you are competing for new business against other people. It sets you apart from the crowd—because most people are not as candid as they should be about what they have done or can do.

■ The Magic of Commitment

Commitment is magical. It is what transforms a promise into reality. It is the energy, the electrical current that is needed to make things happen. It is the power to change the face of things. Commitment is not easy—it is making the time when there is none, finding resources when there seem to be none, it is overcoming what appear to be impossible obstacles. It is the daily triumph of integrity over skepticism. It is coming through time after time, year after year after year.

Commitment is choosing to be effective and about saying, "I will find a way to make this happen." It is about being out there, exposed, vulnerable, even subject to ridicule, because intensity is often considered bad form. Commitment also has its rewards—it is feeling good about yourself because you know you are being true to yourself and your word. It is what brings a light to our faces and our lives.

■ Maturity Is a Multitude of Things

Maturity is many things. First, it's the ability to base a judgment on the big picture—the long haul. It means being able to pass up the fun-for-the-minute and select a course of action which will pay off later. One of the characteristics of infancy is "I want it now." Grown-ups are able to wait.

Maturity is the ability to stick with a project or a situation until it is finished. Maturity is the ability to face unpleasantness, frustration, discomfort, and defeat without complaint or collapse. The mature person knows he or she can't have everything his or her way. Nobody "wins 'em all." The mature person is able to defer to circumstances, to other people, and to time.

Maturity is the ability to do what is expected of you, and this means being dependable and reliable. It means keeping your word; it means personal integrity. Do you mean what you say, and do you say what you mean?

The adult world is filled with people who can't be counted on. They never seem to come through in the clutch. They break promises and substitute alibis for performance. They show up late—or not at all. They are confused and disorganized. Their lives are mazes of unfinished business. Their behavior suggests a lack of self-discipline—which is a large part of maturity.

Maturity is the ability to make a decision and then stick to it, riding out whatever storms may follow. This requires clear thinking, backed with the courage to stand by your position once you've taken it. Immature people spend a lifetime exploring possibilities and doing nothing. Action requires courage. And courage means maturity.

Maturity is the ability to harness your abilities and your energies and do more than is expected of you. The mature person refuses to settle for mediocrity. He or she would rather aim high and miss the mark than aim low and make it. Where do you fit in?

■ The Silence Between the Words

Yes, people can listen to the words that are spoken, but are they hearing what is being said? Someone is telling you how excited she was on her vacation. Before she is even finished, you are either thinking of your own vacation, or of questions to ask about her vacation, or even drifting off to some other topic. Were you into her feelings? Were you into her experience? Were you into where she was coming from?

A friend once said, "If you agree with what I am saying, then it is not that you agree with me, but that I agree with your theories. Conversely, if you disagree with what I am saying, then it is not that you disagree with me, but that I disagree with your theories." Do you get the message? The secret to communicating is not to agree or disagree. It is to hear what is being said, without any type of judgment. Once you begin to insert your ideas into the picture, you are no longer hearing but interpreting what is being said. Real communication requires no interpretation.

One of my most influential teachers was my mother. One day she was telling me about some of her problems, some of her feelings, some of her perceptions of her life. I began offering advice. I began suggesting ways she could view her world that would result in less negativity. I began playing the therapist's role. After a few minutes she stopped me cold. She said, "I don't want your advice or help. I did not ask for any of your garbage. All I want is for you to listen to me, to what I am saying and feeling!" What a slap in the face that was! All I could say was, "Thank you," and for the first time I began to actually hear what she was saying and what she was not saying. What she was not saying was much more important than what she was saying. I thank God that she gave me the opportunity to hear and not just listen.

Too often we listen to the words, but we do not hear what is being said. If one simply stops the mind for a few minutes and lets communication occur, the hearing happens. In fact, when the mind stops working so hard, even the message that existence is sending will be heard. The music, the meaning, the flow can finally be heard. No thinking is necessary to hear what is being said. The meaning will come in as clear as a bell.

Communication is not about words! Communication is about the transmission of ideas! Communication is the flowing of existence. Yes, words are important when conveying ideas and thoughts, but the real message goes far beyond the words: It is the silence that is found between the words and between the thoughts.

Do this the next time you are in the middle of an argument with someone—sit down, hold hands, look the other person in the eye, and let the communication happen. This might take real courage, real strength, real trust, but it will be well worth the effort. It may take a little while to let the mind rest, to let the thoughts disappear, to let the ego evaporate. Only by letting go will what is really important have the opportunity to be expressed. Not the expectations, the desires, the wants, the hopes, but the feelings. The communication then is of one being with another. The communication is not even of two beings but one essence in two bodies. Put the mind aside and enjoy the communication with nature, with existence, and with yourself.

■

Pearls of Wisdom

Great is the man who does not lose his child's heart.

—Mencius

■

Much of your pain is self-chosen. It is the bitter potion by which the physician within you heals your sick self. Therefore, trust the physician, and drink his remedy in silence and tranquillity.

A man is not honest simply because he never had the chance to steal.

The purpose of life is not to be happy. The purpose of life is to matter, to be productive, to have it make some difference that you lived at all.

Let him go where he will, he can only find so much beauty or worth as he carries.

—Ralph Waldo Emerson

■

Those things are dearest to us that have cost us the most.

—Michel de Montaigne

■

Those undeserved joys which come uncalled and make us more pleased than grateful are the ones that sing.

—Henry David Thoreau

■

■

Spirit and matter are inseparably one in every aspect of the universe. The body is our visible spirit. It is the miracle of spirit made manifest.

—*Yogi Amrit Desai*

■

■ Personal Truths of Louise Hay

1. The subconscious mind does not have a sense of humor. It takes everything you say at face value. So don't belittle yourself, don't criticize, and don't talk about what you don't want to happen.

2. It is vital that we forgive. This has nothing to do with condoning bad behavior, but we need to be willing to forgive so we do not destroy ourselves and so we can be set free.

3. If there is one thing we can all drop, it is criticism. Criticism of ourselves or another person keeps us stuck where we are. If we can come to a place of acceptance and self-love, it is easier to make changes. You are not making the change because you are a bad person and are doing things wrong. You make changes because you love yourself and you want to improve the quality of your life.

The Art
of Being You
—

Even when walking in a party of no more than three, I can always
be certain of learning from those I am with. There will be good
qualities that I can select for imitation and bad ones that will teach
me what requires correction in myself.

—Confucius

CHAPTER

4

Understanding commitment and fulfillment would be far easier if most of us were not misled by the juvenile interpretation of the pursuit of happiness that is so widely held today. Gratification, ease, comfort, diversion, and a state of having achieved one's goals do not constitute happiness for human beings.

Despite our most frantic efforts, happiness in the form of total gratification is not a state to which people can aspire. The irony is that we should bring such unprecedented dynamism to the search for so static a condition.

More sensibly, some of us in recent years have come to a conception of happiness that differs fundamentally from the storybook version. The storybook conception tells of desires fulfilled. The truer version involves striving toward meaningful goals—goals that relate the individual to a larger context of purposes. Note that we speak of happiness as striving toward meaningful goals—not necessarily attaining them. Storybook happiness involves every form of pleasant thumb-twiddling. True happiness involves the full use of one's powers and talents. Both conceptions involve love, but the storybook version puts greater emphasis on being loved, while the truer version emphasizes the capacity to give love.

Thus, thoughtful people are almost certain never to conclude that they have "arrived." People are by nature goal-striving beings. And because we are built this way, we are not happy unless we function as we were meant to—as purposeful seekers. You and I are seekers on a sacred, ancient path carved out by trailblazers like Buddha, Mohammad, Jesus, Moses, the great yogis, gurus, medicine chiefs—countless men and women of every age, race, and land. We happen to be keepers of the precious torch for truth in this age.

Wisdom and joy come only from learning to see a wider, much more wondrous world. Power comes only from the spirit within. This is why most of us feel weak, lifeless, and weary to the bone. We drag ourselves around just trying to make it through each day, often pausing to wonder whether good times in life are worth all the effort and pain.

What I've been exploring is changing my vision. And the change begins with a look at the two worlds that I inhabit at the same time—the outer world of appearances and the inner world of spirit. From the world of appearances, life may look very different from one minute to the next, or from one age to the next. But from the big view—from the world of the spirit—there is only one process going on. We are born, we have good times and bad, we experience a wide range of emotions, we face various problems and challenges that make us feel good or bad about ourselves, we learn some things and forever wonder about others, and then we move into the unknown. Life for each of us is truly just this one story.

It's easy to see that most of us aren't yet playing with the spiritual advantage that's been given to us. We haven't yet gotten tired enough of the hustles and hypes. We haven't yet reached upward and inward for the truth of how life works or why we struggle so hard. So much fear! So much desire! Do we really have anything to lose by going after bigger stakes?

■ Symptoms of Inner Peace

■ *A tendency to think and act spontaneously rather than on fears based on experiences.*

■ *An unmistakable ability to enjoy each moment.*

■ *A loss of interest in judging other people.*

■ *A loss of interest in interpreting the actions of others.*

■ *A loss of interest in conflict.*

■ *A loss of the ability to worry. (This could be a very serious symptom.)*

■ *Frequent overwhelming episodes of appreciation.*

■ *Contented feelings of connectedness with others and with nature.*

■ *Frequent attacks of smiling.*

■ *An increased tendency to let things happen rather than to make them happen.*

■ *An increased susceptibility to the love extended by others as well as an uncontrollable urge to extend it.*

—Hede Marker

■ How to Get the Most Out of Yourself

Your success in business, sports, friendship, love—nearly every enterprise you attempt—is largely determined by your own self-image. People who have confidence in their personal worth seem to be magnets for success and happiness. Good things drop into their laps regularly, their relationships are longlasting, their projects are usually carried to completion. To use the imagery of the English Romantic poet William Blake, they "catch joy on the wing."

Conversely, some people seem to be magnets for failure and unhappiness. Their plans go awry; they have a way of torpedoing their own potential successes, and nothing seems to work out for them. Problems such as these usually stem from a difficulty with self-acceptance. Once they are able to gain more confidence, these people often find their troubles take care of themselves. I believe that anyone can change his or her self-perception. A person with a low self-image is not doomed to a life of unhappiness and failure. It's possible to get rid of negative attitudes and gain the healthy confidence needed to realize one's dreams. Here are some thoughts on how this can be accomplished:

■ *Focus on your potential, not your limitations.* When Helen Hayes was a young actress, producer George Tyler told her that were she four inches taller, she could become one of the great actresses of her time. Miss Hayes recalls, "I decided to lick my size. A string of teachers pulled and stretched till I felt I was in a medieval torture chamber. I gained nary an inch—but my posture was military-straight. I became the tallest five-foot woman in the world. And my refusal to be squelched by my limitations enabled me to play Mary of Scotland, one of the tallest queens in history." Helen Hayes succeeded because she chose to focus on her strong points, not her weak ones.

Many people think that, because they are not as smart or good-looking or witty as others, they are inferior. Probably no habit chips away at our self-confidence quite so effectively as that of looking at the people around us to see how we compare. And when we find that someone is indeed smarter, better looking, or wittier, we feel our self-worth diminish. The Hasidic Rabbi Zusya was asked on his death bed what he thought the kingdom of God would look like. He replied, "I don't know. But one thing I do know. When I get there, I am not going to be asked, 'Why weren't you Moses? Why weren't you David?' I am only going to be asked, 'Why weren't you Zusya? Why weren't you fully you?'"

■ *Devote yourself to something you do well.* There is nothing so common as unsuccessful people with talent. Usually the problem lies not in discovering your natural aptitudes, but in developing those skills. Young surgeons practice skills for months on end, skills like tying knots in confined places or suturing. The refining of these abilities is the surgeon's main method of improving total performance. Many of us get interested in a field, but then the going gets tough. We see that other people are more successful, and we become discouraged and quit. But it is often the boring, repetitive sharpening of our talents that will ultimately enable us to reach our goals.

Somewhere under the stars God has a job for each of us to do, and nobody can do the task better. Some of us must find the place by trial and error. Success can take time, with dead ends along the way. But we should not get discouraged because others seem to be more skilled. Usually the deciding factor is not raw talent but practiced skill.

■ *Learn to silence the self-criticism in your head.* Have you ever noticed how many negative statements you make to yourself? Most people converse with themselves in a negative manner. "My hair looks terrible this morning." "That was a stupid remark I made; she probably thinks I'm a dummy." Since thousands of messages flash through our brains every day, it is small wonder that the result is a diminished self-image. Why not use affirmations to replace this barrage of negativity?

Start with one simple affirmation, such as "I am enough" or "I am perfect just the way I am." Repeat this affirmation ten or fifteen times a day, preferably while looking in the mirror. Say it aloud where appropriate, and silently during elevator rides or while standing in line at the bank. You'll be amazed at how concentrating on the positive can begin to improve your self-image.

■

How to Be Really Alive!

Live juicy.
Stamp out conformity.
Stay in bed all day.
Dream of Gypsy wagons.
Find snails making love.
Develop an astounding appetite for books.
Drink sunsets.
Draw out your feelings.
Amaze yourself.
Be ridiculous.
Stop worrying.
Now. If not now, then when?
Make yes your favorite word.
Marry yourself.
Dry your clothes in the sun.
Eat mangoes naked.
Keep toys in the bathtub.
Spin yourself dizzy.
Hang upside down.
Follow a child.
Celebrate an old person.
Send a love letter to yourself.
Be advanced.
Try endearing.
Invent new ways to love.
Transform negatives.
Delight someone.
Wear pajamas to a drive-in movie.
Allow yourself to feel rich without money.
Be who you truly are and the money will follow.
Believe in everything.
You are always on your way to a miracle.
The miracle is you.
—Sark

■

■ Living with Abandon

Several years ago, I received a postcard from Jackson Hole, Wyoming. It read, "I am skiing with abandon!" I wondered what my friend meant. I surmised that he was skiing skillfully, joyfully, peacefully, and with confidence. Although I have no hopes of skiing at that level, I have great hopes and dreams of living with abandon—skillfully, joyfully, peacefully, and with confidence. I believe successful men and woman through the ages have captured the four secrets of living with abandon.

■ *You must have a self you respect.* This means having a deep sense of responsibility for your thoughts and actions. It means keeping your word, being counted on to deliver, and remaining faithful to yourself, your family, and your work. When you respect yourself, you believe in what you are doing and you work hard, for work adds flavor to life. You set your own standards rather than comparing yourself to others, for each individual has his or her unique talents. Respect for self means not worrying about who gets credit but doing the job well.

It's not a question of being better than someone else; respect and integrity demand that you be better than you thought you could be. Having a self you respect means knowing with quiet confidence that you will choose what is right and not waver from your chosen course of action when criticized.

■ *You must have a commitment to the lives of others—your family, friends, and colleagues.* You must learn to be an encourager, thinking and saying cheerful and pleasant things, believing in others, taking time to nurture others' dreams. A wise man once said, "If you want one year's prosperity, grow grain; but if you want ten year's prosperity, grow men and women." You can show your commitment to the lives of others by providing the nutrients of gratitude and encouragement—i.e., by investing your time and energy in their aspirations and worthy goals.

■ *You must learn to consider setbacks as windows of opportunity.* People who learn to live with abandon have discovered that personal trials make them more sensitive and loving; that inconveniences build endurance and character; that irritants are not excuses for failure but obstacles to be overcome. These wise folks know that achievements worth remembering are stained with the blood of diligence and etched with the scars of disappointment. They have learned what Churchill meant when he said, "Never give up—never, never, never!"

Perhaps you have heard the saying, "Life doesn't do anything to you, it only reveals your spirit." The pages of history are filled with heroic stories of men and women who triumphed over disabilities and adversities to demonstrate victorious spirits. Bury him in the snows of Valley Forge and you have a George Washington. Raise him in abject poverty and you have an Abe Lincoln. These individuals adjusted to difficulties to make their greatest weaknesses their greatest strengths.

■ *You must learn to enjoy life's process, not just life's rewards.* We live in a goal-oriented society where problems are resolved not in the future but right now. We want three-minute oatmeal, one-hour dry cleaning, overnight success. We care nothing for the process; we want only to arrive. But individuals who would live with abandon must learn to enjoy the process, not just the reward.

I believe this means living one day at a time, savoring the little victories, and realizing that life is an endless journey of self-discovery and personal fulfillment. Living the process means knowing that Rome was not built in a day, nor does a career alone make a life worth living. Other ways of living the process include petting the cat, hugging the kids, thanking the secretary, or simply letting the other fellow get ahead of you on the freeway.

■ Feeling Good About Yourself

I have been spending more time alone—quiet and reflective time in which I can listen to my thoughts and reflect upon the day and myself. Right now, it is high noon, mid-August, and as I write, I am sitting in the cool Colorado air, enjoying the magnificent scenery of the Rocky Mountains.

My friends, this is a wonderful space to be in—loving ourselves, appreciating ourselves, trusting our feelings. While it is important to be centered on yourself, it is also important to be aware of your effect on other people. When it comes to following your higher vision, to doing those things that serve humankind, take a stand that is compassionate and gentle. After all, what we all want in life is to feel healthy in body, mind, and spirit—and to be excited about life.

Sondra Ray, in her book *Loving Relationships,* says, "People treat you the way you treat yourself. If you love yourself, you will automatically give others the opportunity to love you. You must become the right person rather than *look* for the right person."

I'm beginning to figure out that if I want "something," I must create nurturing conditions without time limits for that "something" to manifest itself. For example, in a garden, we do not grow flowers. Rather, we create the conditions in which flowers can grow. If I want carrots, I've got to plant carrots. If I want radishes, I've got to plant radishes. If I want love, I've got to plant love. If I want understanding, I've got to be understanding.

■ My New Friend

Daring to be alone in his company I knew not what to expect—he bid me first to take leave of the office, clients, and money issues. Into the full sun of the day he pulled me.

Oh so tolerant of whims, sensitive to my every need, he gave me permission to do just about anything, pampering me, expecting nothing in return.

As I ran down the bike trail pretending to be a wild bird, he clapped; as I wrote the newsletter, he rewarded my words with smiles and nods.

To think I might not have dared to be alone in his company (against me he could have turned at any moment). It was boredom, panic, and loneliness I had risked, when he was there for me all along.

The very best friend in the world—myself.

—Tom Feltenstein

■ Self-Love and the Way of Nature

Surely you have noticed how some days go quite well, and others seem to deteriorate from the moment your feet hit the floor. Many variables could account for such divergent directions. Yet it's more than likely that how you feel about and relate to yourself is a powerful determining factor in the way your day unfolds.

According to the laws of nature, all of your relationships with the world are mirrors of your relationship with yourself. If you are in harmony and aligned with yourself, the chances are great that you will experience harmony, joy, and fulfillment in your outer world. I know that many of the problems in my life occur when my love of self is scarce. I believe the same is true for so many others whose problems are directly related to their inability or unwillingness to love themselves.

We seem to fight, alter, or avoid who we are through unacceptance and disapproval of self. We sit in constant judgment of ourselves, ready to try, convict, and hang at dawn. In the words of the cartoon character Pogo: We have met the enemy and they are us. How you relate to yourself determines how and what you eat, the amount of sleep you get, whether or not you wear seat belts, how much exercise you get, and whether or not you drink alcohol, smoke, or take drugs.

Self-love is simply your own approval of the way you are. Self-love means being uncritical, understanding, and kind to yourself so that you can relate to the world with the same compassion. If you are happy with you, if your relationship with the outer world works, then your life will be filled with joy. You need self-love because:

■ You can't receive love from others if you can't love yourself. If someone says, "I love you," your brain replies, "I don't deserve it." To paraphrase Groucho Marx: How could you be part of an organization that would have you as a member? You don't deserve it. Then again, the group can't be all that great if they invited a nothing like you to be a member.

■ You can't give love to others if you can't love yourself. Giving love to others creates the fear that you will run dry. It's the fear of scarcity again. The more you give away, the less you'll have. Of course, nothing could be further from the truth when it comes to love. What you give out in love comes back to you a thousandfold.

■ You'll be controlled by negative emotions that stem from the lack, or scarcity, of self-love. For example, defensiveness, anger, fear, and depression all germinate in a loveless soul.

■ You'll be controlled by limiting negative thoughts about yourself. Lack of self-love permits you to accept such beliefs as true, never to be questioned or changed.

With self-love, you can do it all. I remember a cartoon of a shiny steam locomotive with a smile on its face as it hauled one hundred cars up a steep hill. The engine proudly exclaimed, "Anything is possible when you feel good about yourself."

■

The Love Within You

Why is it that intelligent, successful, and even gifted people become dissatisfied with their lives? Many outwardly successful and seemingly well-balanced people secretly suffer from nagging feelings of discontent—even emptiness.
The answer is love. In the long run, material success and social

*status are less important than the marvelous spirit of love within a
person. The ability to be fully human and to love others is vital to
personal growth and happiness.
And it is vital to career growth as well. Learn how to express
yourself honestly and lovingly and you'll invariably increase the
level of trust on the job as well as with friends and family. You'll
grow as a leader, as a communicator, as a decision maker.*
—*Author unknown*

■ Emotional Rescue

Your emotions have a powerful effect on your health, according to a world-famous medical specialist. "Feelings rule our mental and physical well-being," says psychiatrist Dr. Vernon Coleman. "My research shows there are ten basic emotions—five negative and five positive. If you can learn to control the negative and strengthen the positive, you'll be well on your way to a happier, healthier, and even slimmer life." Here are the five positive traits you should cultivate:

■ *Laughter:* Laughter really is the best medicine. When you laugh, you release healing hormones inside your body, your blood pressure drops, breathing is easier, and you sleep better.

■ *Hope:* We all need our dreams, otherwise life is hollow and unrewarding. Try recalling the goals and ambitions you had when you were a teenager and see how many of them you can revive.

■ *Love:* Dr. Coleman notes that love is a miracle cure. His files are full of cases where love prevailed after medicine had failed.

■ *Optimism:* Every time you hit one of life's snags, look on the bright side. Training yourself to see the glass half full instead of half empty will ease a troubled mind and body.

■ *Confidence:* Unless you learn to assert yourself, you will be pushed around while you seethe inwardly with unspoken replies. Stand up for yourself!

And here are the five *negative* emotions you should avoid like the plague:

■ *Anger:* Hidden anger can cause high blood pressure, heart attacks, strokes, and stomach ulcers. If you feel anger rising, do something physical. Beating carpets or taking a brisk walk can do wonders.

■ *Fear:* We're more afraid of the unknown than anything else, so learn as much as you can about what frightens you. It will lose its negative power over you.

■ *Boredom:* Inactivity can cause heart disease, bowel problems, skin troubles, and depression. Get up and get going!

■ *Sadness:* If you feel sad, cry. Crying helps the body rid itself of harmful wastes and wards off depression.

■ *Guilt:* This is a major cause of stress-related illnesses like headaches and stomach ulcers. Tell yourself, "I'm only human; I make mistakes."

■ Planting Seeds

Think for a moment of a tomato plant. A healthy plant can have more than a hundred tomatoes on it. In order to get this tomato plant with all these tomatoes on it, we need to start with a small dried seed. That seed doesn't look like a tomato plant. It sure doesn't taste like a tomato plant. If you didn't know for sure, you would not even believe it could be a tomato plant.

However, let's say you plant this seed in fertile soil, and you water it and let the sun shine on it. When the first tiny shoot comes up, you don't stomp on it and say, "That's not a tomato plant." Rather, you look at it and say, "Oh boy! Here it comes," and you watch it grow with delight. In time, if you continue to water it and give it lots of sunshine and pull out any weeds, you might have a tomato plant with more than a hundred luscious tomatoes. And it all began with that tiny little seed.

It is the same with creating a new experience for yourself. The soil you plant in is your subconscious mind. The seed is the new affirmation. The whole new experience is in this tiny seed. You water it with more affirmations. You let the sunshine of positive thoughts beam on it. You weed the garden by pulling out the negative thoughts that come up. And when you first see the tiniest little evidence, you don't stomp on it and say, "That's not enough!" Instead, you look at this first breakthrough and say with glee, "Oh boy! Here it comes! It's working!" Then you watch it grow and become a manifestation of your desire.

Creed for Happiness

I shall begin each morning unafraid, and shall seek the wonderful gift that the day will bring me. I shall be guided by intelligence rather than belief, and shall see truth and ignore no fact. I shall control my thoughts and guide them into the highest realm, holding my cherished ambitions and sacred ideals uppermost in my mind. Throughout the day I shall enjoy all the beauty of my surroundings. I shall glory in my associates and aspire to the exaltation that comes with love of God and mankind. I shall forgive freely before forgiveness is asked. I shall harbor ill thoughts toward none. I shall fulfill every trust. I shall remain poised and serene in every trial, and face each emergency without fear.

I shall be friendly and courteous toward all. To me each day will be one of kindly deeds and unselfish love. I shall obey those in authority and give loyalty to all to whom it is due. I shall be clean in body, action, and thought. I shall revere my God and have the utmost respect for the religious convictions of my fellows.

To obtain the most from life I shall give the best that I can give. At all times will I enthrone service and eliminate the motive of gain. I shall perform each task cheerfully. I shall build and not destroy.

And so will I come to the end of each day with the satisfaction brought by service, serenity, kindness, and love. I shall go to my rest with the peace that comes from an untroubled mind and the memory of tasks well done.

—*Author unknown*

■ How Rich Are You?

You are richer today than you were yesterday:

■ If you have laughed often, given something, forgiven more, made a new friend, or turned stumbling blocks into stepping stones.

■ If you have thought more in terms of others than of yourself, or if you have managed to be cheerful even when you were weary.

You are richer tonight than you were this morning:

■ If you have taken time to trace the handiwork of God in the commonplace things of life.

■ If you have learned to count things that really don't count, or if you have been a little more forgiving of the faults of friend or foe.

You are richer:

■ If a little child has smiled at you and a stray dog has licked your hand.

■ If you have looked for the best in others and have given others the best in you.

■ The Science of Happiness

Happiness, a perennial subject of interest to philosophers, songwriters, poets, and most of us in general, has recently come under scientific study. The results, so far, suggest that many traditional beliefs of the past have been incorrect. Some research indicates that a happy childhood is not the key to adult happiness. Dr. Jonathon Freedman, professor of psychology at Columbia University, found that people who had "very unhappy childhoods—whose parents divorced or died, who were treated cruelly or coldly, who had physical or psychological problems—still managed to be happy adults, by and large."

To further muddy the waters, it was found that many people who appear to have every good material circumstance going in their favor and have every reason for joy and light-heartedness are, more often than not, dissatisfied or angry. They are quick to flare up at the slightest circumstance that does not sit right with them.

Happiness, studies show, is less predictable than we had formerly suspected. Dr. Freedman points out, "People quickly get used to whatever they have, good or bad, and only when changes occur from the level to which they're adapted are the emotions we call happiness or unhappiness produced."

The three most damaging factors to our psyches are fear, doubt, and guilt. When we allow any of these three to reign over our emotions, we invite unhappiness. The opposites on the positive side of the ledger are confidence, self-assurance, and a clear conscience. Those who habitually treat others with kindness, empathy, understanding, and thoughtfulness—who treat others as they would love to be treated themselves, who remember birthdays and anniversaries and do those little things to show appreciation of others, be it spouse, neighbor, or even the boss at work—are the people usually found to be in tune with positive emotions and that elusive spirit we call "happiness."

■ Bottled-Up Good

You and I have an enormous amount of good bottled-up inside us waiting to be let out. It takes time and effort for us to discover the great good we have going for us. Unfortunately, we have not been taught how to effectively discover and put to use the creative good for our own benefit. I am convinced that too many of us have developed "stinking thinking" about our "good" potential—about the good we do and are capable of doing, about the good we can create and the good around us. We have been raised on such garbage as: "Oh, look out ... don't do that." "You are naughty. You should be ashamed of yourself." "Why can't you be like Jimmy or Betty?" "You're a fool. Be careful." "Be afraid." "Life's tough people are out to get you. Get them first." My gosh! We just keep being fed negatives about good: "But you don't understand. You're stupid." "You shouldn't ... you can't do that!"

As the negative junk is continually thrown at us, it becomes increasingly difficult for our minds to picture our ability for good or even greatness. Our "stinking thinking" produces insecure feelings in us that tend to color our lives today.

There is a great deal of inner stress and pain that goes along with such feelings, which in turn zaps our energy, enthusiasm, spontaneity, confidence, creativity, courage, and mental well-being. We allow those feelings to control our lives, and as a result, we allow our lives to get out of balance. We keep our good from expanding, and we attract little good toward us.

We become more preoccupied with our belief in our badness than our belief and faith in our innate goodness. We dwell on thinking narrow thoughts about just how good we really are. We allow ourselves to get drawn into inconsistencies, contradictions, and difficulties—mostly of our own making. As we struggle through the maze of daily choices with which we are confronted, dissatisfaction, frustration, and unhappiness grow because the good and greatness we see in others seems to escape us.

But the good bottled up in you is powerfully strong. Begin to tap into it and put it to use in your "now" life. You are as good as anyone. Take away the negatives—reveal the positive by making statements against your fears or your imagined badness. Get clear on a positive and hold onto it consistently. Love yourself and watch what happens.

■

A Winner Says ...

For positive expectations:
A winner says, "I was good today. I'll be better tomorrow."
A loser says, "With my luck, I was bound to fail."

For motivation:
A winner says, "I want to! I can do it!"
A loser says, "I have to. I can't."

For self-image:
A winner says, "I see myself changing, growing, achieving, winning."
A loser says, "They're my hang-ups, faults, and stupidities, and
I'm stuck with them."

For direction:
A winner says, "I have to plan to make it happen. I'll do what is
necessary to get what I want."
A loser says, "I'll try to hang in there—muddle through somehow."

For self-control:
A winner says, "I'll take the credit or the blame for my performance."
A loser says, "I can't understand why life did this to me."

For self-discipline:
A winner says, "Of course I can do it! I've practiced it mentally a
thousand times."
A loser says, "How can you expect me to do it? I don't know how!"

For self-esteem:
A winner says, "I do things well because I'm that type of person."
A loser says, "I'd rather be somebody else."

For perspective:
A winner says, "I live every moment, enjoying as much, relating as much, doing as much, giving as much as I possibly can."
A loser says, "I'm only concerned with me today."

For self-awareness:
A winner says, "I know who I am, where I am coming from, and where I am going."
A loser says, "Who knows what I could do if I only had the chance."

For receptiveness:
A winner says, "Tell me what you want. Maybe we can work on it together."
A loser says, "There's no point in discussing it. We're not even on the same wavelength."

Let's all go out and apply these winning attitudes. When better is possible, good is not enough!

■ Ten Ways to Win

Since a good self-image is important to any endeavor, let me share with you ten points I believe will help you develop a healthy self-regard.

■ *First:* Make others feel important by listening to them. Eventually you will find that they will in turn make you feel the same.

■ *Second:* Accept yourself as you are, but be open to change for the better. Changing yourself from who you are to who you want to be can save your life.

■ *Third:* Do something for others every day. This is a great way to feel good about yourself.

■ *Fourth:* Learn to accept compliments as your due. Never belittle what others find good about you.

■ *Fifth:* Use your individuality as an asset. Don't become a conformist. Most of life's great achievers were iconoclasts who listened to their inner voice.

■ *Sixth:* List your past successes and refer to that list often—especially when you are down.

■ *Seventh:* Set clear, reachable daily goals, but make them flexible, too.

■ *Eighth:* In life's race, do not compete with others but only with your own past record.

■ *Ninth:* Use affirmative language. You can't think positive thoughts while speaking negative words.

■ *Tenth:* Have a positive self-development plan going at all times. Read, listen to, and attend anything available pertaining to a positive mental attitude.

■ The Neglected Art of Being Different

One of the most vivid and painful recollections of my life concerns ... a hat. When I was eleven, my parents sent me to a summer camp run along semi-military lines. Part of each camper's uniform was supposed to be a Boy Scout hat, low-crowned, wide-brimmed, to be worn every afternoon without fail when we lined up for formal inspection. But my parents did not provide me with a Scout hat. Through some catastrophic oversight, they sent me off with one of those army campaign hats, vintage 1917. It was wide-brimmed all right: When I put it on, I was practically in total darkness. Whenever I wore this hat, instead of being an inconspicuous (and somewhat homesick) boy, I became a freak.

Or so I thought. Looking back now, across the years, I can smile at the memory of my wan little face peering out forlornly from under that monstrosity of a hat. But it was not a joke at the time. I was miserable—utterly, abjectly miserable. Why? Because I was different—different from the others, different from the crowd.

The fear of being different, like most fears, tends to diminish when you drag it into the light and take a good look at it. At the bottom of such fear lies an intense preoccupation with self. That comical hat, back in my childhood, might have caused some momentary merriment or temporary teasing. But the whole thing was too trivial to have lasted long. I was the one who kept the moment alive by agonizing about it.

It takes courage to be different, but there is also an art to it—the art of not antagonizing people unnecessarily by your differences. People don't object to differences nearly so much as they object to the attitude of superiority that so often goes with it. The rule of thumb is very simple: Be as different as you like, but try to be tolerant of the people who differ from you. If we all granted one another the right simply to be ourselves, we would be different enough. When Henry David Thoreau was eight years old, someone asked him what he was going to be when he grew up. "Why," said the boy, "I am me! I will always be a second-best somebody else. I am the best me there is!"

■ You Are What You Believe About Yourself

One day a naturalist who was passing by inquired of the farmer why it was that an eagle, the monarch of all birds, would be persuaded to live in the barnyard with chickens.

"Since I have given it chicken feed and trained it to be a chicken, it has never learned to fly," replied the farmer. "It behaves as chickens behave, so it is no longer an eagle."

"Still," insisted the naturalist, "it has the heart of an eagle and can surely be taught to fly."

After talking it over, the two men agreed to find out whether this was possible. Gently the naturalist took the eagle into his arms and said, "You belong to the sky and not to the earth. Stretch forth your wings and fly."

The eagle, however, was confused; she did not know who she was. Seeing the chickens eating their food, she jumped down to be with them again. Undismayed, the naturalist took the eagle the following day up on the roof and urged her again, saying, "You are an eagle. Stretch forth your wings and fly." But the eagle was afraid of the unknown and jumped down once more for the chicken food.

On the third day the naturalist rose and took the eagle out of the barnyard to a high mountain. There he held the monarch of birds above him and encouraged her again, saying, "You are an eagle. You belong to the sky as well as the earth. Stretch forth your wings now and fly." Then the eagle began to tremble; slowly she stretched her wings. At last, with a triumphant cry, she soared to the heavens.

It may be that the eagle still remembers the chickens with nostalgia; it may even be that she occasionally revisits the barnyard. But she has never returned to lead the life of a chicken. Just like the eagle, if you have learned to think of yourself as something you aren't, you can redecide in favor of what you really are.

■ The Power, the Joy, and the Art of Self-Love

Self-love is acknowledging yourself for deciding to journey on the path of self-discovery. Self-love is investigating with a sense of curious interest your intuitive, creative urges—those that are not grounded in logic or reason. Self-love is remembering with a sense of relief that already encoded in your genes are your purpose, your talents, and the means to your fulfillment, and that you are naturally guided toward that fulfillment when you praise, compliment, and appreciate yourself.

Self-love is challenging any limiting concept about yourself and others while knowing that the truth of your unlimited nature will reveal itself to you. (And it will.) Self-love is knowing, with a sense of power, that the quality of all your experience is the result of what you affirm life to be, knowingly and unknowingly. Self-love is appreciatively acknowledging people you feel kindly and loving toward as a demonstration of the love you have for yourself.

■

The Bottom Line

So, you've dabbled in the occult, burned candles, given up sex.
You've traveled to Sedona to visit the vortex.
You've meditated, visualized, affirmed with love and grace.
You've forgiven all your irritants till you're blue in the face—
You've been "est"-ed and you've tested tarot and astrology.
You've met your guides from the other side
and did past-life therapy.
So, you've been Rolfed and hypnotized,
there's nothing you've avoided.
You've tried acupuncture, heavy breathing,
even been Sigmund Freuded.
You've chanted mantras and you've om'ed and journeyed near
and far—
You've seen many of the channels and taken every seminar.

You've floated in a tank and have gone the psychic route—
You've had your cards and wrinkles read,
did primal scream to shout—
You burn incense in the afternoon, sometimes reflex your feet.
You've become a vegetarian and very seldom cheat—
You gave up salt and sugar and your diet's really pure.
Although at times you still get gas, just why you are not sure.
You drink herb tea until you see the best in all at last.
Your Kundalini's straightened and no longer at half mast—
You've had your aura cleaned and your chakras lubed and tuned.
You've seen E.T. at least four times and two times for Cocoon—
You go to sleep with crystals and you wake up with a tape
that subliminally instructs you, to get your mind in shape—
You've gone here and there and everywhere,
tried everything you know.
The path that's called Enlightenment is such a busy show—
So much to do and see and know, there are so many places
for you to go so you are sure to cover all the bases—
But after all that's said and done and all the things you've tried,
there is a truth that you should know, while you are on your ride—
The light you see that all seems to be coming from the things you do
is only as bright as is the light that radiates from you.

—Author unknown

■

■ Enlightenment

I would like to propose that you are an actor or actress. You have been practicing your whole life. You have been mastering a role known as you. I don't know about you—sometimes I get tired of playing a role that long. You have played it so long that you begin to believe that you are the role—as if you were hired to be in a movie. You were hired to be a villain, or a nice person, or an accountant, or a law-enforcement officer, or a yuppie, or whatever role you were playing; and after playing it long enough, it became your reality. And you became such a method actor that you forgot it wasn't your reality.

You were just playing that role.

Well, suppose, just suppose, you were hired to play a law-enforcement officer. They said, "Well, we could only pay you one hundred thousand dollars, but would you be willing to do it?" And you said, "Well, let me think about it—yes." So what's the first thing you do, if you're going to be a good actor or actress, which is truly a transcendental art? Wouldn't you go out and study what it's like to be a law-enforcement officer? Wouldn't you learn to model on them?

You see, you were a master of imitation when you were little. That's how you learned to talk and do many other things. But then, when you were still young, someone called you a copycat, and your talent for imitation probably started falling off at that point, but it is a wonderful way to learn. Modeling is a more sophisticated form of copying. You don't just characterize or mimic somebody, or caricature them. You get inside them. You say, "What do they think like, what do they feel like, how do they walk?" You literally put yourself in their shoes.

So, if you were really going to do a good job of playing a law-enforcement officer, you might ride around in a police car for a while—right? And then you'd go out with them after hours and see what brands of beer they drink, if they drink. You'd see what kind of church they attend, what they do on the weekend, how they get along with their spouse (if they're married), what kind of clothes they wear when they're off duty, what kind of food they eat. You'd really learn about them, and you'd start eating that stuff and doing those things, and you'd feel inside what it's like. You are not trying to become somebody. You are being them. That's what modeling is. So that's what you would do if you were going to play the role of a law-enforcement officer.

But what if somebody said, "Hey, now we have another job for you. It is only for five minutes. It is the role of an enlightened being." Well, you say, "All right, gee whiz, I'll go for it." Now, the first thing you do is you want to model on somebody, but there aren't too many people around who are enlightened beings. Or maybe there are and we just haven't noticed.

Enlightened beings can play any role. They can act any way they want, but their quality is naturally more loving. Are they happy or sad? Happy, right? Are they focused or diffused? Probably focused. Are they relaxed or tense? Relaxed. Do they breathe shallowly or deeply? Probably slowly and deeply. You see, we all know what it is like to be enlightened. You know how to play the role. So you model on that—that image in your heart. It is like,

"Thy will be done." You know the feeling, whether you're comfortable with that phrase or not.

So you get before the camera, and they say, "Roll 'em," and you sit relaxedly or you get up and move across the room gracefully, soothingly, in no hurry. And you have a beatific smile on your face, or maybe something happens and you're angry, but you totally let it go. You let it flow. You let it go, and you go on for a while playing this role—a natural being, ordinary, happy, loving—and then finally after what seems an eternity, they yell, "Cut," and you go, "Whew, I'm glad that's over," with a new appreciation.

Well, what if they never yelled, "Cut"? The secret of enlightenment—and the practice of enlightenment—is to have the heart and the courage to play the role of an enlightened being past the end of the movie. That's it. It's the most simple and natural process in the world, yet it's complex, because it involves every area of your life. Everything turns into a contemplation.

You get up in the morning and ask yourself, "How would an enlightened being wake up?" You sit up and begin moving toward the bathroom. You ask yourself, "How would an enlightened being walk? What does an enlightened being do in the bathroom, and how does he or she do it?" And you see what answers come, and you gradually adapt.

You are going to work, and someone cuts you off on the highway, and you say, "Whoa—oops." You are playing the role of an enlightened being and you can't resist totally. What would an enlightened being do? Now, don't make yourself a caricature. There are bad actresses and actors who caricature police officers, and they act in a way they think they should, but they're just mocking or mimicking. What would an enlightened being really do? Maybe they would yell out at the person freely, without attachment to what he or she was saying, or maybe they would just release it and bless the driver. Who knows? But you act according to what's in your heart.

You get to work and you say, "What would an enlightened being do at work?" How would an enlightened being relate to other people, or in a marriage situation, or with a boyfriend or girlfriend? What would his or her business dealings be like? How would an enlightened being eat? Exercise? What time would he or she go to bed? You see, life becomes a total contemplation. Not where you get up in your head and think all about this, but you begin to adapt; life develops what it demands. It depends what standards you want to work.

If your image of being an enlightened person involves being perfect—

never making any mistakes—well, you are going to have a real interesting time being enlightened. You will probably constantly be judging yourself. But the moment you notice yourself judging, you say, "Wait a minute. Do enlightened beings judge themselves all the time? Are they hard on themselves? Nah, they must be forgiving. Are they humorous? Sure." And little by little, you adapt to that practice because life develops what it demands. It doesn't mean you have to blissfully tolerate situations that aren't very good.

So, sometimes an enlightened being might choose to change circumstances. If you are willing to practice it, you can bet you will feel a little like I did when I started running. People kept telling me to relax, not to use all the muscles I had. I was used to using strength and that kind of force. They said relax, and it was very frustrating. I felt like I was tighter than I had ever been in my life. You know what? I wasn't really tighter. It just felt like it.

In light of the demand to stay relaxed, it made me more conscious of how tight I'd been. Like sunlight over a well, I began to see in the light of that demand all the little creepy crawlies. That's why it seems to get worse before it gets better. That's why it seems darkest before the dawn. So in the face of that practice, if you're willing to do it and are interested in doing it, you'll seem more enlightened than ever. But understand, that's not true. You are just beginning to increase your self-observation naturally—not judgmentally, but naturally. And the beginning of strength is awareness of weaknesses.

-

Today

Starting now, I will begin this day anew,
with the thought of becoming the person I'd like to be;
if not completing that difficult journey today,
at least getting it a little further along the way.

Today I will set aside some time just for me ...
to plan, to dream, to be honest with myself and about myself;
to become better acquainted with this person that I am,
and this place that I call home.

Today I will experience something new.
I will learn from the world around me,
from the words I read, the sounds I hear,
the touches I feel, the faces I see.
Even through the course of my daily tasks,
I will try to lean toward understanding,
try to make the commonplace a wondrous place to be.

Today I will think of my friends
and be warmed by the thought
of my loved ones,
and try to show them all the love that I feel.

Today I'll thank the people and places
that have helped me along on my way,
the friendships and smiles, the hardships and trials,
that have made me what I am today.

Today I'll remember how naturally happiness comes
to the person who thinks it should be.
I'll remember how—by some interesting twist—
doing for others is also doing for me.

I'll remember that having a sense of humor
has helped me to survive.
I'll remember how when everything else seems to go wrong,
that I'm glad of life, of living this day ...
I'm happy to be alive.

Today I will listen to my inner needs
and comply as best I can:
with a little learning from my mind;
as much love as my heart can hold;
nourishment and exercise for my body;
seeing all the beauty of the world for my soul.

Today I will think of the past
only long enough to learn from it;
the future only for a fleeting dream.
Today is my day; this minute is mine ...
I'll make it work for me.
—Author unknown

■

Pearls of Wisdom

Love yourself first and everything else falls into line. You really
have to love yourself to get anything done in this world.
—Lucille Ball

■

It is in the enjoyment and not in mere possession that makes for
happiness.
—Michel de Montaigne

■

For he who gives joy to the world is raised higher among men than
he who conquers the world.
—Richard Wagner

■

Everyone's life is a fairy tale written by God's finger.
—Hans Christian Anderson

■

Ah, but a man's reach should exceed his grasp, or what's heaven for?
—Robert Browning

■

A laugh is worth a hundred groans in any market.
—Charles Lamb

■

You never find yourself until you face the truth.
—Pearl Bailey

■

■

Nobody can make you feel inferior without your consent.
—Eleanor Roosevelt

■

■ Personal Truths of Terry-Cole Whittaker

1. Love yourself with all your heart, soul, and mind. Love others as you love yourself.

2. Live your dream, your vision, in a way that supports the well-being of all life.

3. Be responsible for creating your own life to be the paradise it can be right here on earth. Create your life to be as beautiful and loving as you desire it to be. Know it is up to you.

Change

—

Unless we change our direction, we are likely to end up where we are headed.

—Chinese proverb

CHAPTER 5

In this time of change—personal as well as global—many of us are creating jobs and businesses that more truthfully express our life purpose. That move takes a daring leap of faith, when it appears that we have abandoned security for the sake of self-expression. As we follow our creative mind into a life of fulfillment based on the rules of a new age, our rational mind reminds us of—and frightens us with—the rules. As a result, some of us journey forward and others do not. Business, in particular, is considered anti-spiritual for most seekers of truth: Trying to fit money into an Eastern and Western synthesis of values is confusing and frustrating. Over the last few years, I've come to realize that the business world is the greatest area for personal transformation. In business, you have to face your fears, transcend your ego, and learn to live beyond limits, all while doing your best to hear and heed the call from within. The payoffs and risks are greater, too. In business, you can grow rich. But you can also end up broke and miserable.

How you respond to events in the business world are tests of strength and wisdom. And the tests come in many forms—divorce, profound burnout on the job, and the inner desire to dump everything we've worked for and uproot, move, and try another road. But following the inner voice doesn't guarantee immediate material success. I'm sure each of you reading this book has faced severe disappointments and humiliating setbacks. And though the setbacks have been difficult at times, right now I am personally prepared to trust my new friend, the inner voice within me. And I believe that the spiritual path has to be workable on a material plain to be valid.

The path of discovery leads us through the marketplace of the world as well as through the desert. I'm learning to trust my feelings, my ideas, and, equally important, what a feeling is. Sometimes those feelings are strange, but in most instances they are profound. I'm letting my rational self make decisions in my daily life. Slowly, and sometimes very painfully, I'm learning to trust a new way of knowing; I'm gradually becoming aware that I can listen to and follow my desires and passions. I believe the way forward comes simply from following what excites me, and as I follow, I slowly become aware that the clues appear more and more often. I'm gradually becoming aware of a subtle agenda that's guiding my life. I'm being led to an opening of my heart—learning to let go of fears and discovering that underneath the worst nightmares is a realm of loving security, a wholeness I've never known existed. I know now that there is no need to separate business from spirituality. They work quite well together. I need only listen to my inner messages. I also know that resisting these signals only postpones and unsettles what might have been a relatively smooth transformation. And instead, a mere tremor is magnified into a major earthquake.

I remember Ram Dass telling a group of businesspeople that if they ignore their inner promptings to change, those nudges will turn into something more attention-getting—like ulcers. So I'm continually listening to the gentle warning of the voice within. Perhaps you might like to do so as well.

■ The Best Way to Manage Change

To organize a change team, you need to look for:

■ *An inventor*—who serves as a top executive and focuses on the broad picture, thereby identifying opportunities for change.

■ *An integrator*—who makes sure plans for change don't disrupt important functions in the company and who consolidates support for change among the employee ranks.

■ *An expert*—who acts as a project director in implementing the plan for change. He handles all of the technical aspects of the change, making sure they're understood by managers and subordinates.

■ *A team of managers*—who delegate new assignments to employees and ensure that transitions to new ways of doing things are completed.

■ Oh, How Time Flies

Several years ago, my family gathered together for a weekend. We met at one of those resort restaurants where the menu is written on a blackboard held by a chummy waiter, and we had a wonderful time. When dinner ended, the waiter brought the check and set it down in the middle of the table. That's when it happened. My father did *not* reach for the check. In fact, my father did nothing.

Conversation continued. I waited and waited, until finally it dawned on me. *Me!* I was supposed to pick up the check. After hundreds of restaurant meals with my parents, after a lifetime of always thinking my father was the one with the bucks, things had changed. I reached for the check and whipped out my charge card. My self-view was suddenly altered. With the stroke of a pen, I was an adult.

Some people mark off their lives in years, others in events. I am of the latter school, and I think of some events as rites of passage. For instance, I did not become a young man at a preordained age, like thirteen. My coming of age was much later, when a kid strolled into the store where I worked and called me mister. I turned around to see whom he was addressing. He repeated it several times: "Mister, mister," looking me straight in the eye. The realization hit me like a punch. He was talking to me. *I* was a mister.

There have been other milestones, and I remember them all. One occurred when I noticed that policemen seemed to be getting younger, not to mention smaller. Another came when I suddenly realized that I was older than every single NFL player I admired. Instead of being big men, the players were big kids. With that milestone went the fantasy that some day maybe I could be a player—not a football player, of course, but certainly a big-league baseball player. As a kid I had a good eye (not much power, but a keen eye), and I always thought I could play the game. One day I realized I couldn't. Without ever having reached the hill, I was over it.

For some people, the ultimate milestone comes with the death of a parent and the realization that you have moved up a notch. As long as your parents are alive, you stay a kid in some way. At the very least, one person remains who loves you unconditionally. One day you go to a friend's wedding. In no time, you celebrate the birth of your friend's kids. And what seems like weeks later you see the kids driving along the street with kids of their own in the back seat. One day you meet at parties, the next at weddings, then at funerals. It all happens in a few days. Take my word for it.

I thought I would never prefer staying home to going to a party, but now

I find myself passing up the late evening. I never thought I would prefer watching athletics to playing them, but the sidelines feel pretty comfortable today. I never thought I would fall asleep in front of the TV the way my friends' fathers did, but the eleven o'clock news seldom sees me awake.

One day I knew what to say to a demanding client. One day I knew how to handle a head waiter. One day I bought a house. One day—what a day!—I became a father. Not too much later I picked up the check for my own dad. Not until I got older did I realize that that day in the restaurant was not just a milestone for me. It was one for my father, too.

■ Steps for Living with Change

Be patient with yourself. The temptation is almost always to get a transition over with as quickly as possible—and it never seems to work. There are eight steps to this process that need to be completed, so you will have to be gentle with yourself. There is something of value to be learned at every stage. You'll move fastest if you don't rush. Much gets stirred up during a transition—emotions, behaviors, relationships, lifestyle—that needs time to settle. As with those glass globes with "snow" scenes inside, the more they are shaken, the longer the snow takes to settle. Take it easy.

Don't be afraid to reach out. There are many ways you can get help as you move through big changes. Sometimes you'll just need someone to listen to you. At other times you may need professional help. But whether it's someone to give you a push, someone to provide moral support, someone to go through it with you, or someone who will hold you and love you unconditionally, don't be afraid to ask for the support of others when you need it.

Here are the steps for living with change:

1. Look forward. There's always a desire to hold onto at least part of the "old" situation. For a while, this is okay, but be careful not to get stuck in the memories. Be clear about what you want after "it" is all over, but don't rush the grieving. Both are important. As you move through the transition, find some support and create some continuity in your life. This could be therapy, friendships, hobbies, and/or other activities that keep you feeling positive and optimistic about the future.

2. Stay open-minded. Whatever happens, hold onto your desire to find creative new approaches to old situations. There's always a temptation to stick to old patterns, which could result in your missing opportunities for new learning. If your transition has been "dropped on you," see if you can find the benefits or opportunities that might come with it. If your transition is one you chose, don't be too surprised if you encounter some unexpected emotional hiccups.

3. Be good to yourself. There's no need to play it "tough" during a transition. Spoil yourself, watch your favorite TV shows, take walks, listen to good music, and let yourself go from time to time. Don't be afraid to cry; you'll feel much better than you would if you tried to keep it all shut up inside.

4. Go for walks. There's always so much more to see and so many different ways to get in touch with the deeper parts of being human. Try spending time outside, watching the changing seasons, playing in the park, being at the shore, climbing mountains, enjoying a sunrise or a sunset. Walking leads to many gifts; take time to be alone with nature.

5. Create small successes. Every success will help you move forward. One of the best ways to move ahead whenever you feel stuck is to create a small project for yourself—one that you know you'll complete successfully.

6. Take some risks. It's a great time to try something new. Since you're in transition anyway, why not have a little adventure and do something for the first time? Everything is changing, so why not?

7. Dream a little. The self-fulfilling prophecy is alive and well: If you can dream it, do it. Imagine you have a magic wand and can make the very best of this change. Dream up your perfect outcome, and when the dark days creep in, remember the dream.

8. Celebrate. Every ending is also a new beginning. It is important to celebrate both the ending and the beginning. Plan a trip or a retreat for yourself that will symbolize the completion of your transition.

■ Are You Addicted to Fresh Starts?

Are you missing the satisfaction of seeing things through? Do you love new beginnings? January 1, a pristine page, the promise of love about to be, dawn's early grapefruit on the first day of dieting? Possibly the most delicious word in ... No, wait. Let me start over.

Are you a fresh-start junkie? Bagging the old and embracing the new can be energizing, restorative, empowering. It can also be addictive. Beginnings are exciting, sexy. What's not to adore? Nothing's gone wrong; you have no regrets. Middles are harder to love and harder to pull off. But without them, what happens to momentum, continuity, consequences, growth, change? Middles are where most of life—especially the good stuff—happens. Still, cleaning the slate packs such a rush. What a relief to know we have the brains, courage, heart to remake ourselves! And sometimes, what an act of laziness and cowardice!

Suppose you (and you know who you are) have slipped into unreliability at work. You've been sloppy and late with important projects, and your job is in jeopardy. Starting over where no one knows you is an option (if you can get the recommendations you need). But so is staying and rehabilitating your reputation—fixing the problem instead of just leaving it behind.

The latter strategy would not be a piece of cake. Middles can be hell. But this path will let you trade quick relief for the satisfaction of seeing something through. You'll discover techniques for getting out of a jam that will probably be applicable elsewhere. You'll learn to trust and appreciate yourself. You'll win the respect of people who watched you change. Instead of running from a bad thing, you'll be learning how to keep the bad thing from happening again.

Suppose salvaging your current relationship seems out of the question. Resentments are too deep-rooted to weed out, you think, and your history too heavy a weight. So you'll start over, and the next partner, a more suitable soul mate, will be the beneficiary of what you know now. But maybe your old partner won't seem so unsuitable if you stick around and see this person under new circumstances. Sure, working out the relationship may involve agony and confrontation. But it may also involve a real and happy change.

Look, I'm not saying that starting over is always bad, or that staying the course is always good. Pack it in or stick it out? That's a tough call. How can you know when it's smart and brave to cut your losses, and when that route is a cop-out? I guess you ask yourself questions. Are you abandoning a relationship, a job, a hobby, your budget, therapy, or tennis lessons because you've given your all and you're positive this won't work? Or is it because you've hit a boring plateau or a painful rough patch? Have you gathered all the information, done all the observing you need in order to make a good decision? Have you given yourself time to know what you feel? Have you given the problem your best shot? Your best 2,782 shots? Is starting over what you always do when the going gets tough?

It's easy in this wacky modern world to become confused about what's disposable and what isn't. Starting over is a very American thing to do. Our nation was founded and flourished on that very principle. One coast gets screwed up, and quicker than you can say Manifest Destiny, folks light out for the territories instead of fixing up the colonies they've despoiled. The wonderful part of that American tradition is that hope springs eternal. The dark side is that we never learn to hang in there. We miss the joy of watching ourselves change over time. We miss the chance to gather information vital to our happiness. I'm not saying you should let your hair grow to your knees or never burn your bridges. These are your choices. Just make sure you are starting over for the right reasons. And consider the pleasure of a story with a happy middle.

■ Eight Ways to Bounce Back from Defeat

When winners fail, they get up and go again. And the very act of getting up is victory.

Winners follow Winston Churchill's advice: "Never, never, never give up." They try and try again. How they achieve this state of mind is an interesting question. Is their secret sheer willpower, stubbornness, natural grit, discipline? The answer seems to be all of the above, and one more thing. Winners repel discouragement by embracing eight go-again attitudes.

1. Winners view failure favorably. As Robert Allen says, "There is no failure, only feedback." Failure is successfully discovering something that doesn't work. It's a learning experience. Winners see in failure a stepping stone. This gives them the desire to get up and go again. Losers see in failure the finality of a tombstone. This causes them to lose heart and quit.

2. Winners keep their expectations realistic. A mountain climber doesn't leave base camp and begin his or her ascent toward the summit of Mount Everest only to quit after a few steps. He or she keeps the goal in perspective. The climber knows that reaching the top requires many thousands of steps, and maybe hundreds of slips. Winners know that reaching their goals requires time and effort. They don't expect to get there overnight. They are mentally prepared to strive over the long haul. They expect to fail and get up many times along their journey.

3. Winners vary their approach. Brian Tracy, in his tape series, *The Psychology of Achievement,* tells of four men who became millionaires by the age of thirty-five. Each was involved in an average of seventeen different ventures before he found the business that made him rich. Losers usually make the same attempts over and over again until they become discouraged and quit. Winners, however, make many different attempts at success. If one approach doesn't work, they are not depressed and they do not blindly repeat the failed effort. Instead, they go again from another angle.

4. Winners create or embrace "have-tos." Famous military leaders have inspired their troops to great accomplishments by burning their boats or their bridges. This tactic proves that necessity is the mother of achievement. People who have to, do! But when getting up is an option, it is very easy to stay down, and that is exactly what a loser will choose. The late Dick Gardner said, "By and large, you will do what you have to do; not much more and not much less." Gardner suggested that debt was a way to create a "have-to" for yourself.

5. Winners find and develop a goal that pulls. A goal without a burning desire to achieve the result is like kissing your sister (or your brother). You'll do it when you have to, but you probably won't knock yourself out for the privilege. How can you create desire? The Bible says, "Where your treasure is, there will your heart be also." Invest the treasure of your time in your goal. Think about it. Write it down in detail. Visualize yourself enjoying the rewards of your goal. Hang up pictures of it. Talk about it. Soon your heart will crave the desired result. And should you fail along the way to your goal, your desire will cause you to jump up and go again.

6. Winners reject rejection. People who try again and again do not base their self-worth on their performance. They have an internally based self-image. They do not tell themselves, "I am a failure." Instead they say, "I missed that opportunity, but I am still a winner!" And when winners fall down and are on the ground, they know that it is not their home. So they get up and go again.

7. Winners enjoy and value the effort. They see work as its own reward. Everybody enjoys commission checks and other payoffs, but a persister enjoys the experience and the challenge of a job well done. As someone said, "If money is your only reward for your work, then you are vastly underpaid, no matter how much money you make."

8. Winners budget their efforts. They know which obstacles to overcome and which to go around. Some salespeople continually lock horns with headstrong prospects until they wear themselves out and have no heart left. Others act like professional visitors and never get past a very timid close. Neither is a successful strategy. Winners—those who continually get up and go again—have found a balance. They are strong closers but don't wear themselves out on one prospect. As Kenny Rogers sings, "You gotta know when to hold 'em and know when to fold 'em."

These eight attitudes are not spontaneous. They are not standard equipment for human beings. You must diligently cultivate and develop these principles. You must knead them into your thoughts and into your daily practice. Only then will they empower you to get up and go again.

■ Maturity

Maturity is the ability to control anger and settle differences without violence or destruction. Maturity is patience; it is the willingness to pass up immediate pleasures for long-term gain.

Maturity is perseverance, the ability to sweat out a project or a situation in spite of heavy opposition and discouraging setbacks. Maturity is the capacity to face unpleasantness and frustration, discomfort and defeat, without complaint or collapse.

Maturity is humility. It is being big enough to say, "I was wrong." And when right, the mature person need not experience the satisfaction of saying, "I told you so." Maturity is the ability to make a decision and follow through. The immature spend their lives exploring endless possibilities and doing nothing.

Maturity means dependability, keeping one's word, and coming through in a crisis. The immature are masters of the alibi. They are conflicted and disorganized. Their lives are a maze of broken promises, former friends, unfinished business, and good intentions that never materialize.

Maturity is the art of being at peace with what we cannot change, having the courage to change what we know should be changed, and having the wisdom to know the difference.

—Author unknown

■

Pearls of Wisdom

The thing you resist is the thing you need to hear most.
The best way out is always through.
—Robert Frost

■

I have never seen a person grow or change in a constructive
direction when motivated by guilt, shame, and/or hate.
—William Goldberg

■

When a man is willing and eager, God joins in.
—Aeschylus

■

Being entirely honest with oneself is a good exercise.
—Sigmund Freud

■

An optimist goes to the window every morning and says,
"Good morning, God." The pessimist goes to the window and says,
"Good God, morning."
—Anonymous

■

The world that we have made as a result of the level of thinking
we have done thus far creates problems that we cannot solve at the
same level we created them.
—Albert Einstein

■

■

Consider how hard it is to change yourself and you'll understand
what little chance you have of trying to change others.

—*Jacob M. Braude*

■

■ Personal Truths of Anne Wilson Schaef

1. Life is a process. I am a process. If I honor and trust my process, I am one with the universe. As I honor my process, I find myself honoring the process of others.

2. There is no transformation without recovery, and there is no recovery without transformation.

3. The practical should always be in service of the important.

4. I wouldn't miss life for anything!

Your Family and Personal Relationships

—

Some day, after mastering the winds, the waves, the tides, and gravity, we will harness for God the energies of love. And then for the second time in the history of the world, humankind will have discovered fire.

—Pierre Teilhard de Chardin

Human contact is one ingredient necessary to our well-being that cannot be mass-produced, packaged, and stored for future use. It rests, instead, on the willingness of each of us to sacrifice spontaneously our time, our pleasures, so that someone else may enjoy the companionship without which life generally loses much of its meaning. All the miracle drugs, instant foods, and inventions of modern science cannot replace the warmth, the comforting handclasp, and the expression of interest and concern of a fellow human being which so much brighten lonely days and ease aching hearts.

How do you foster human intimacy? It is really quite simple.

1. Speak to people. There is nothing as nice as a cheerful word or greeting.

2. Smile at people. It takes seventy-two muscles to frown, only fourteen to smile.

3. Call people by name. The sweetest music to anyone's ears is the sound of his or her own name.

4. Be friendly and helpful. If you would have friends, be friendly.

5. Be cordial. Speak and act as if everything you do is a genuine pleasure.

6. Be genuinely interested in people. You can like everybody if you try.

7. Be generous with praise, cautious with criticism.

8. Be considerate of the feelings of others. It will be appreciated.

9. Be thoughtful of the opinion of others. There are three sides to a controversy—yours, the other person's, and the truth.

10. Be alert for opportunities to give service. What counts most in life is what we do for others.

And remember, there is a saying that really speaks of the value of friendship: If you have a clear conscience and good health, if you have a few good friends and a happy home, if your heart has kept its youth and its soul and its honesty, then cheer up—you are still one of life's fortunate millionaires.

■ Start Within

John Lennon said, "Life is what happens while we're busy making other plans." I've been running so hard and pushing people along for the ride. I've lost perspective—what's life really all about? What is success?

It's time to turn inward—*my peace, health, and joy are right here, right now.* What am I chasing after? There's no place to go but right here. Now! If I want to learn something, I've got to teach it. I need to be gentler during my lectures. I need to call into my talks bigger things, like *kindness, patience, courage, and honesty.*

I feel so spiritually clumsy—out of balance, running from one city to another, one meeting to another. Why? I tell myself to "chill out" and to let life in the fast lane be replaced by life in the *vast* lane. A mind that is open, free of fear, free from unwanted thoughts, will be clear and powerful enough to deal with anything. Truth requires openness. In order to become more powerful, we have to start letting go of our attachments and our constant busyness. That stuff is like sand in the gas tank. With so much noise, hype, fear, and desire bombarding us all day long, it might take a lot of daily practice to help us spot the truth within and around us. But what else is there to do—live like suckers, shucking and jiving and lying to ourselves all our lives, feeling secretly weak and disconnected from this incredibly beautiful world we could have held in our immense hearts?

Calm down, be still, and turn inward to the God who dwells deep inside. Don't get carried away by things that glitter, just love everyone and take courage, for God is always with you.

■ A Mystical Secret

Each of us has the starring role in this great movie. We're all heroes, adventurers who have a lot of ups and downs. We may stumble and fall a million times, but we can become strong, wise, and free by the end. It's really a very beautiful story. The "outer" world of appearances—what we usually call reality—is nothing more than a prop room. It contains everything that operates under the law of time. Think about it: No matter what we ever get or have, we won't be able to hold on to it for very long. Our possessions, our greatest inventions, even the wonders of nature and our own bodies are merely props. We use them for a while, but then the parts rust, the paint peels, the flesh sags, the heart stops, the earth quakes. What time brings us, time takes away. It's all part of the deal.

Whenever I hold on to my anger, I turn small stuff into really big stuff in my mind. I start to believe that my positions are more important than my happiness. They are not. If I want to be a more peaceful person, I must understand that being right is almost never more important than allowing myself to be happy. The way to be happy is to let go and to reach out. Let other people be right. This doesn't mean I'm wrong—everything will be fine. I'll experience the peace of letting go as well as the joy of letting others be right.

■ Are You a Goose?

When you see geese flying along in a V formation, you might be interested to know what science has discovered about why geese fly that way. It has been learned that as each bird flaps its wings, it creates an uplift for the bird immediately following. By flying in a V formation, the whole flock adds at least seventy-one percent greater flying range than if each bird flew on its own. Similarly, people who share a common direction and sense of community can get where they are going more quickly and easily because they are traveling on the draft of one another.

Whenever a goose falls out of formation, it suddenly feels the drag and resistance of trying to go it alone, and quickly gets back into formation to take advantage of the lifting power of the bird immediately in front. If we have as much sense as a goose, we will stay in formation with those who are headed the same way we are going.

When the lead goose gets tired, he rotates back and another goose flies point. It pays to take turns doing hard jobs—with people, or with geese flying south. The geese honk from behind to encourage those up front to keep up their speed. What do we say when we honk from behind?

And finally, when a goose gets sick or is wounded by a gunshot and falls out, two geese fall out of formation and follow it down to help and protect it. They stay with the goose until it is able either to fly again with another formation or to catch up with the group. If we have the sense of a goose, we will stand by each other like that!

—Author unknown

■ Relationships

One of the things that goes on in most of our relationships is an attempt to control each other's behavior, especially when we are not together. We demand that our partner be a certain way. Boy, how true! I propose a new kind of agreement: When I am not with my partner, I will conduct my life in a way that supports my ability to be with my partner when I am with her. When I am not with my partner, I will not do things that will interfere with my ability to be with her when I am with her.

In other words, when I am not with her, I will conduct myself in the adventure of life in such a way that when I am with her again, the time I was not with her will have become a foundation for a deeper experience of well-being and even more enjoyment when we are together.

And if there are certain lessons that she has to learn when I am not in a position to support her in learning them, she needs to be free to go where she will get that support. A relationship should not suppress our adventure or the speed with which we learn the lessons that are there for us to learn. Our experience of being apart can totally support our experience of being together.

■ Labels

We put labels on life all the time—right, wrong, success, failure, lucky, unlucky. This may be a limiting way of seeing things. Labeling sets up expectations of life that are often so compelling that we can no longer see things as they really are. These expectations often give us a false sense of familiarity with something that is new and unprecedented. We begin to establish relationships with our expectations rather than with life itself. Belief traps us or frees us; labels can become self-fulfilling prophecies. We may be as wounded by the way in which we see an illness as by the illness itself, forgetting that *a diagnosis is an opinion and not a prediction.*

I know that I'm the most difficult person I have to deal with. If I can love Tom, I can love all my fellow human beings. I got the idea from Dr. Bernie Siegel to keep pictures of myself as a child around to help me recall what a precious creation I am and to remind me to be more forgiving of myself. Like Bernie, I ask all the people I have relationships with to help keep me on track and to forgive me when I'm not. My family does a good job of keeping me on track. When I received a special award, my son Andrew helped out by observing, "I guess they've lowered their standards."

Not long ago, my wife, Kathy, and I were sitting side by side on the sofa discussing an upcoming speech I was going to give, and I said, "You're impossible." Kathy responded, "No dear, I'm next to impossible." She is right, and I love her, so now I accept seventy-five percent of the responsibility for our relationship, and I am working my way up. After all, Joseph Campbell and my wife agree: Marriage is an ordeal and a struggle because you are creating a relationship, a new entity, devoid of self-interest.

Time isn't money, it's everything. Spend it on who and what you love.

■ Love or Infatuation?

Infatuation is instant desire. It is one set of glands calling to another. Love is friendship that has caught fire. It takes root and grows—one day at a time. Infatuation is marked by a feeling of insecurity. You are excited and eager but not genuinely happy. There are nagging doubts, unanswered questions, little bits and pieces about your beloved that you would just as soon not examine too closely. It might spoil the dream.

Love is quiet understanding and the mature acceptance of imperfection. It is real. It gives you strength and grows beyond you to bolster your beloved. You are warmed by his or her presence, even when he or she is away. Miles do not separate you. You want him or her near, but near or far, you know the other person is yours, and you can wait.

Infatuation says, "We must get married right away. I can't risk losing him." Love says, "Be patient. Don't panic. Plan your future with confidence." Infatuation has an element of sexual excitement. If you are honest, you will admit it is difficult to be in one another's company unless you are sure it will end in intimacy. Love is the maturation of friendship. You must be friends before you can be lovers.

Infatuation lacks confidence. When the other person is away, you wonder if he or she is cheating. Sometimes you check. Love means trust. You are calm, secure, and unthreatened. He or she feels that trust and it makes him or her even more trustworthy. Infatuation might lead you to do things you'll regret later, but love never does. Love is an upper. It makes you look up. It makes you a better person than you were before.

■ How to Mend a Broken Heart

A broken heart can cripple your entire life—but only if you let it. The prognosis doesn't have to be terminal if you follow a healing process that will turn your emotional pain into a positive experience. Thankfully, a pair of top therapists have designed a concrete plan to help mend the agonizing heartbreak of being dumped by a loved one. In the highly acclaimed book *Lifemates: The Love Fitness Program for a Lasting Relationship,* psychiatrist Harold M. Bloomfield and his counselor wife, Sirah Vetese, Ph.D., have compiled a list of critical dos and don'ts for those suffering from a broken heart:

■ Do stay calm. Don't panic. Try to remember that you will heal, that the pain will not last forever. Think of all the people you know who have survived similar losses. You will too.

■ Do recognize and accept your hurt. Don't deny it. Feeling the pain and desolation of emotional trauma is a normal stage in healing. Realize that you'll be stronger for having endured the pain.

■ Do rest and nurture yourself. Don't stay isolated or use alcohol or other drugs. Rest is a good prescription for any injury, be it physical or emotional. Extra sleep will help fight off depression. But locking yourself away or trying to numb the pain with chemicals will only prolong your suffering.

■ Do take care when making important decisions. Don't make impulsive judgments. Remember, your thinking is clouded by trauma. You'd be wise to postpone major decisions until you're further along in your recovery. If you must make an important choice, seek advice from friends or counselors.

By following these and other helpful guidelines in their book, Bloomfield and Vitese say you can transform your emotional pain into personal growth. As they point out: You need to heal a broken heart completely and learn what you can from the experience.

■ Forgiveness

I now believe—as do many therapists—that true adulthood arrives with the capacity to forgive. By forgiveness, however, I do not mean the willingness to excuse someone else's obvious or assumed guilt for the sake of magnanimity or simply to "get past the past." I'm increasingly convinced that mature forgiveness is primarily an act of surrender—the willingness to relinquish some of our most cherished and defensive beliefs about reality itself. This forgiveness may include releasing others from blame—and the emotional catharsis that brings—but it spreads far beyond that, as it calls out one's own ego-based definitions of how things and people really are.

For people who are not used to considering philosophical questions—and who consequently accept the version of reality passed on by society and advertised by its media—forgiveness can be doubly difficult. It first requires accepting responsibility for one's own perceptions and admitting that we do not all see the world the same way. A particular person's view of the world at any moment is significantly colored by transitory emotions, recalcitrant prejudices, and deep complexes from personal traumas. For many, this realization would be a major philosophical achievement, requiring a degree of introspection that our society generally finds suspect. But the second step toward real forgiveness—the willingness to surrender our most fundamental prejudices—is a great challenge indeed.

■ On My Son's Thirteenth Birthday

My son, Andrew, became a teenager on February 15, 1990. At the threshold of his entering this fascinating and tempestuous stage of life, I felt a real passion to express fatherly sentiments. With Andrew's permission, I'd like to share a letter I wrote to him:

Dear Andrew:

On the eve of your thirteenth birthday, I wanted to share a few moments with you. To tell you I am proud of you would be an understatement. I am so pleased that we found each other thirteen years ago. I know that whatever you do will be a big win for you—in the business world, in the personal relationship world, in the sports world, in the spiritual world.

Most important, I want you to have fun, and I want you to have compassion for your fellow human beings. Learn to enjoy the simple pleasures of life. Enjoy what you already have ... you have a great deal to be grateful for. You have brought so much joy into my life. I treasure the times we spend together.

Andrew, start taking the time to learn from your life experiences and spend less time trying to figure them out. You have so much energy—direct it in ways that are productive and meaningful to your personal growth. Remember, too, that there are many kinds of leaders. There are silent leaders, leaders of armies, leaders of a select few. The one thing these men and women have in common is a deep trust in their instincts and personal vision. Andrew, you are a leader. You lead in a unique way that only Andrew Feltenstein can, and I know you will have the strength to trust your instincts in the face of life's temptations.

Andrew, you are so full of action, so alive, I know that someday you are going to share that energy and live fully with others.

Laugh a lot, love a lot, and don't be afraid to cry and be vulnerable. Life is an exciting adventure. Take full advantage of all it has to offer. Finally, son, respect others, act happy, feel happy, be happy.

I love you more than words can express.

As we go through this journey called life, we are all going to make mistakes. That is how we learn. We are all in training, and life can sometimes be difficult, but what an opportunity! The light will disturb us when we are comfortable and comfort us when we are disturbed. Trust yourself and trust the process that is your life. It has been said that there is one journey but many paths. Here's wishing you happiness on your own path, on the journey without distance we travel together.

I love you,

Dad

■ It Takes an Honest Effort to Teach Kids to Tell the Truth

I told a white lie the other day, and my children, ever vigilant, took me to task. "Dad!" the older one said as soon as I hung up the phone, "Your nose is growing as long as Pinocchio's." He might have been right. No matter how I tried to explain that this lie was necessary—after all, why worry my sister about something she can't do anything about?—my words served no purpose. Their faces remained grim, and I felt duly chastised. Next time I'll be more careful not to get caught.

Honesty is one of those qualities that, taken to the extreme, can verge on the tactless and the cruel. Yet it is something we value and admire, and rightly so. Honesty is perhaps the most important element of integrity.

I am trying to raise my children to be honest in an imperfect world, in a world where cheating is commonplace and, in certain cases, encouraged and lauded. We lie on our income taxes, inflate expense reports, and goof off on the job without thinking twice about whether or not these actions are right. Everybody does them, don't they?

As a matter of fact, honesty is so uncommon—particularly among the rich and famous, and especially when a lot is at stake—that people who choose to be honest make headlines. We are taken aback by their daring, by their oddness, and, yes, by their naïveté. Don't they know better?

Several years ago, tennis sensation Jennifer Capriati said that a ball hit by her opponent was in, despite a lineman's call to the contrary. She did this twice. Her opponent was given the points. Later she told reporters she wanted to be fair and to "Just say the shot was good because it was good." In the passion of the competition, with $100,000 and a sports car at stake, I'm not sure I would have done the same thing.

In Palm Beach, Jennifer Ann Hawkins returned a handbag she found while jogging. There was $2,600 in cash and a pouch of precious jewels worth tens of thousands of dollars. Would you have acted the same way as this young woman?

Aside from their honesty, Capriati and Hawkins have another thing in common. They were both young—fourteen and eleven years old, respectively. This does not surprise me. Actually, it fills me with hope. Cynicism may still not have tainted the young. It's a tricky concept, teaching children to tell the truth. Their worlds are black and white. They don't pull any punches. It is difficult to explain that an occasional fib is necessary. It's hard to explain why it's not nice to proclaim in an elevator, "Boy, Dad, that lady's fat!" even if she is.

Since getting caught by my kids the other day, I have taken great pains to differentiate the black lies from the white. I am not sure they understand. The social lies we tell to protect are not the same as the ones we tell to save our necks. Variations of the latter, told consistently and without remorse, eventually lead to self-deception. These are perhaps the saddest and most tragic of lies, because they indicate that we have lost touch with ourselves, with that annoying little voice that nudges our conscience.

Everyday honesty—returning the extra ten dollars the cashier gave you by mistake—is rarely rewarded. You probably won't make the eleven o'clock news or receive a check from the local civic organization for your good deed. On the contrary, you may even be regarded by those around you as something of an eccentric. Your honesty may ruin the deceit for others.

I don't know how many George Washingtons with cherry trees I'll raise. But the next time I ask, "Who broke the thingamajig?" and I don't hear a chorus of "Not me!" I'll feel I'm doing something right. Honesty, after all, can be measured in infinitely small ways.

■

Give Him a Day

What shall you give to one small boy?
A glamorous game, a tinseled toy?
A Boy Scout knife, a puzzle pack?
A train that runs on some curving track?
A picture book, a real-live pet?
No, there's plenty of time for such things yet.
Give him a day for his very own,
Just one small boy and his Dad alone.
Give him the gift that only you can,
The companionship of his old man.
Games are outgrown and toys decay,
But he'll never forget,
If you give him a day.

—Author unknown

■

■ Cuddled Children Are More Likely to Succeed

Children who are held, cuddled, and showered with hugs and kisses are more apt to grow into successful adults than those who "learn discipline" at an early age, psychologists said recently. Following up studies conducted thirty-six years earlier on a group of five-year-olds in Boston, the researchers said that parental warmth had more influence on adult social adjustment than any other factor.

Although warmth from both parents was significant in a child's ultimate success, the results lent particularly strong support to the notion that a father's manner is important in development. The study compared mothers' assessments of the way five-year-olds were parented in 1951 with the psychological and social well-being of those same children in 1987.

"Adults whose mothers and fathers were warm and affectionate were able to sustain long and relatively happy marriages, raise children, and be involved with friends and recreational activities outside their marriage at midlife," the authors concluded in a report in the *Journal of Personality and Social Psychology.* Children of cold parents were more likely to be depressed and to suffer from a lack of well-being. On the other hand, contrary to the authors' expectations, there was no significant correlation between "difficult childhood" or "parental harmony" and ultimate success.

Original information on the manner in which the five-year-olds were being reared in 1951 was collected by Harvard University psychologists who interviewed mothers and teachers of 379 kindergarten-aged children. Mothers were asked to rate the amount of affection the child received in terms of hugs, kisses, and cuddling. In 1987, psychologists Carol Franz and David McClelland of Boston University and Joel Weinberger of Adelphi University interviewed 78 percent of the group. Their study was the first to look at the long-term influence of parental warmth on the development of social skills in adults.

The "most important finding," the researchers wrote, was a significant association between cases in which mothers had reported parental warmth in child-rearing in 1951 and the child's conventional social accomplishments at age forty-one. "It was especially interesting that father warmth was related to later social accomplishment," they said. "These results provide more support for the notion that a father's contribution to his child's well-being is important."

Legacy of an Adopted Child

Once there were two women
Who never knew each other.
One you do not remember,
The other you call Mother.
Two different lives
Shaped to make yours one.
One became your guiding star,
The other became your sun.
The first gave you life,
The other taught you how to live it.
The first gave you a need for love,
And the second was there to give it.
One gave you a nationality,
The other gave you a name.
One gave you the seed of talent,
The other gave you an aim.
One gave you emotions,
The other calmed your fears.
One saw your first sweet smile,
The other dried your tears.
One gave you up—
It was all that she could do.
The other prayed for a child,
And God led her straight to you.
And now you ask me through your tears
The age-old question through the years;
Heredity or environment—
Which are you a product of?
Neither, my darling, neither,
Just two different kinds of love.

—Author unknown

■ Don't Make Kids' Report Cards a Measure of Their Worth

Okay, it's that dreaded time of year when you know you're up for an evaluation at work. As the hour draws near, you find your palms clammy and your mind distracted. If it's a good evaluation, you feel proud. If it's a bad one, life looks pretty miserable. The last thing you need is to go home and have a family member yell at you about it. But that's just what it's like for your child when it comes time for report cards, says Ann Lynch, president of the national PTA. Four times a year in most schools, report card in hand, kids go home anxious about whether Mom and Dad will like what they see.

"They've got to carry their own stick home," Lynch says. "If they know the parent is unrelenting and takes a strap to them, that's a terrible trip." Report cards are an institution in the U.S., often bearing letter grades from A to F that tell how children are doing in subjects from math to citizenship. Educators urge parents not to overrate the importance of grades, but in reality parents do just that, Lynch says. The results can be violent.

No national studies confirm this, but communities nationwide report anecdotal evidence that child abuse rises noticeably in the days after report cards go home. In Marietta, Georgia, the Cobb County police always suspected a tie-in. "We used to joke around the office: 'Get ready, report cards are coming out,' " recalls Lt. Robert Pittman of the Crimes Against Children unit. But after checking the records, they joked no more: The normal caseload of three to five abuse reports a day would increase by three to eight cases.

In Houston, counselors and police gathered informally to discuss the most stressful times for families. A recurring answer? The arrival of report cards, says Rogene Calvert, executive director of the Houston chapter of the Child Abuse Prevention Council. In response, Houston launched a "Stop the Report Card Reflex" campaign. Its pioneering work was taken nationwide by the National Committee to Prevent Child Abuse in Chicago, which sent information to communities, with tips for parents.

The problem is that parents often take their child's grades personally, as a reflection on their parenting abilities, Lynch says. The grades become tied up with their own expectations for their children's success. "Every parent thinks his or her child is a genius," Lynch says. "It becomes an adult status symbol." But Lynch says a parent "needs to look at a report card as a thermometer rather than as a piece of paper that tells whether the child is wonderful or not wonderful." Here are some parenting tips for those report card days:

- Don't be surprised by them. Lynch says, "I think a parent should keep up all the time with how a child is doing in school and look at his or her homework so that a report card is not a real shocker, either good or bad."

- Learn the teacher's grading schemes. Some grade on a curve, comparing kids with other students in class, some on a kid's "absolute" knowledge of items they should know.

- Don't give monetary rewards for good report cards. Some parents will offer one dollar for each A, five dollars or more for straight A's. The problem is that such rewards are automatic, and some argue that it harms self-motivation.

- Likewise, bad report cards are no reason for punishment. "If you ground your child—or if you yell and scream or tell him he is lazy or stupid— you will be doing nothing to improve his grades, and in fact, you will probably make the situation worse," writes Melitta J. Cutright in "The National PTA Talks to Parents: How to Get the Best Education for Your Child."

If too much TV or too many after-school interests are hurting your child's grades, parents may want to develop a plan to curtail those activities. But they should substitute each hour of time taken away from something with time spent toward improving grades—taking the child to the library, for instance, or working with him or her on problem subjects, says Lynch. Then, when a child shows an improvement in those subjects, it's time for a celebration. Parents can reinforce the behavior by treating the child to something special—a night at a favorite restaurant, for instance. However, "the real reward for a grade is what the child has learned," Lynch says.

■

Pearls of Wisdom

I know some good marriages—marriages where both people are just trying to get through their days by helping each other, by being good to each other.

—Erica Jong

■

■

A good marriage is like an incredible retirement fund. You put everything you have into it during your productive life, and over the years it turns from silver to gold to platinum.
—Willard Scott

■

No man knows his true character until he has run out of gas, purchases something on the installment plan, and raises an adolescent.
—Edna McCann

■

No man can possibly know what life means, what the world means, what anything means, until he has a child and loves it. And then the whole universe changes and nothing will ever again seem exactly as it seemed before.
—Lafcadio Hearn

■

It is one of the most beautiful compensations of this life that no man can sincerely try to help another without helping himself.
—Ralph Waldo Emerson

■

You can make more friends in two months by becoming interested in other people than you can in two years by trying to get other people interested in you.
—Dale Carnegie

■

I expect to pass through life but once. If, therefore, there be any kindness I can show, or any good thing I can do to any fellow being, let me do it now, as I shall not pass this way again.
—William Penn

■

■ Personal Truths of Ann Landers

■ Remember that a child is a gift from God, the richest of all blessings. Do not attempt to mold that child into the image of yourself, your father, your mother, your brother, or your neighbor. Each child is an individual.

■ Don't crush a child's spirit when he or she fails. And never compare him or her to others.

■ Discipline your child with firmness and reason. Don't let your anger throw you off balance. If your child knows you are fair, you will not lose his or her respect or love. Make sure the punishment fits "the crime."

■ A husband and wife should present a united front. Never join with your child against your spouse.

Leadership

Our present crisis calls out for leadership at every level of society and in all organizations that compose it. Without leadership it is hard to see how we can shape a more desirable future for this nation or the world. The absence or ineffectiveness of leadership implies the absence of vision, a dreamless society, and this will result, at best, in the maintenance of the status quo or, at worst, in the disintegration of our society because of lack of purpose and cohesion.

Over the next decade or two, the leadership we are talking about will become more evident in organizations able to respond to spastic and turbulent conditions. We do face an uncertain and unsettling future, but not one without vision. Vision is the commodity of leaders and power is their currency. We are at a critical point in our nation's history, and we cannot go back as individuals or as a country to what we were ten, five, or even one year ago. The future is now and it's our turn.

—Warren Bennis and Burt Nanus, Leaders: Strategies for Taking Charge

CHAPTER 7

Dwight Eisenhower once said, "Leadership is the art of getting someone else to do something you want done because he wants to do it!" Now that's motivation. And motivation for success is contagious, but you have to spread the germ of the idea. Your employees will catch on only when they see your commitment to doing your part.

There are a number of important ways to encourage employee motivation. The first is by destroying the attitude of being afraid to fail, an attitude that produces the minimum level of concentration, initiative, and innovation from people in the performance of their jobs. Winning means being unafraid to lose. This means allowing people to take risks even when they don't always bring home the bacon. If you want progressive, innovative people on your team, you've got to reinforce the risk-taker, not the yes-man.

President Eisenhower, an aide once observed, "could look at people with a smile and get them to do what he wanted." It's a wonderful quality to have. Other things being equal, a friendly, likable supervisor is always more persuasive than one who isn't. There's nothing wrong with a pleasant, good-natured approach to people and problems—in fact, there's none better. The strange thing is that we so often forget to use it. Why?

One reason is that under the pressure of business, we sometimes take ourselves a little too seriously. We get to thinking about our own feelings and problems and forget about the other fellow's. A more subtle reason is that so many people think they have to be gruff or grumpy in order to appear firm and decisive and to get things done. This isn't so.

You can be just as firm and decisive with a smile on your face as you can with a scowl. And just as convincing, too—once people have learned that you have a habit of meaning what you say and following through to make it stick. If you take a minute to think of some of the best bosses you've ever worked for, you probably find that most of them:

- Were approachable and easy to talk to

- Rarely became overexcited or flew off the handle

- Didn't let a few problems poison their whole outlook

- Took a friendly, pleasant approach

- Showed consideration for the feelings of the people who worked for them.

It's no pleasure to work for a disagreeable, grouchy boss. His or her attitude is bound to create feelings of distaste and resentment that sooner or later will have an adverse effect on the performance of subordinates. When it comes to dealing with people, there are very few things that can't be done with a pleasant approach and a smile on your face—and done better because of them.

■ On Leadership

Perhaps the most promising trend in our thinking about leadership is the growing conviction that the purposes of the group are best served when the leader helps the followers to develop their own initiative, strengthens them in the use of their own judgment, and enables them to grow and become better contributors.
—John Gardner

■ Excellence

Excellence is never an accident. It is achieved in an organization or institution only as a result of an unrelenting and vigorous insistence on the highest standards of performance. It requires an unswerving expectancy of quality from the staff and volunteers. Excellence is contagious. It infects and affects everyone in the organization. It charts the direction of the program. It establishes the criteria for planning. It provides zest and vitality to the organization. Once achieved, excellence has a talent for permeating every aspect of the organization.

Excellence demands commitment and tenacious dedication from the leadership of the organization. Once it is accepted and expected, it must be nourished and continually reviewed and renewed. It is a never-ending process of learning and growing. It requires a spirit of motivation and boundless energy. It is always the result of a creatively conceived and precisely planned effort.

Excellence inspires; it electrifies. It potentializes every phase of an organization's life. It unleashes an impact that influences every program, every activity, every committee, every staff person. To instill it in an organization is difficult; to sustain it, even more so. It demands adaptability, imagination, and vigor. But most of all, it requires from the leadership a constant state of self-discovery and discipline.

Excellence is an organization's lifeblood. It is the most compelling response to apathy and inertia. It energizes a stimulating and pulsating force. Once it becomes the expected standard of performance, it develops a fiercely driving and motivating philosophy of operation. Excellence is a state of mind put into action. It is a road map to success. When a climate of excellence exists, all things come easier—staff work, volunteer leadership, finances, programs, etc. Excellence in an organization is important ... because it flows through everything.

■ Creating a Culture of Constant Improvement

Constant improvement (CI) is easy to applaud as a competitive necessity, relatively easy to get started on, but devilishly difficult to implement as a way of life. CI inverts a surprisingly large share of our beliefs about the nature of work. Nonetheless, I have observed firms, large and small, that are making the transition. From these companies, I have extracted a ten-point platform for achieving what I describe as a culture of constant improvement.

1. Make constant improvement strategic. The culture of CI must become what you are all about. Making CI a way of life is as revitalizing as R&D or dramatically altering a firm's market position. Effectively implemented, CI is not a sometimes, for some people, affair. Constant improvement becomes the firm's chief source of sustainable competitive advantage. Some savvy observers have called the commitment to *kaize*, the Japanese word for constant improvement, the biggest difference between Eastern and Western management.

To be strategic, CI must be more than a program. It must seep into every cranny of the firm, be talked up ceaselessly, and dominate the executive team's deliberations and calendars.

2. Approach constant improvement systematically. Don't let CI become a gooey concept. It's amenable to planning and measurement. Each manager (and eventually each non-manager) should have a personal plan that lays out training and time commitments, as well as hard results to be achieved. Progress on such plans should be visibly tracked. Signs of CI (such as charts or displays about improvement projects) should decorate the workplace.

3. Emphasize team as well as individual accomplishments. CI by every person will be best served by creating work teams, both natural work groups and more contrived cross-functional teams. Group enthusiasm and peer pressure are essential to building and sustaining momentum behind CI.

4. Use training. CI is not mysterious or soft. Train in hard topics (statistics, economics, accounting, and problem analysis) and soft ones (interpersonal dynamics and team leadership). CI doesn't come naturally, even though it taps the very natural tendency to want to improve, so long suppressed in the average workplace.

5. Think small. The toughest part of CI for American executives typically hooked on "breakthrough" thinking may be learning to adapt a fetish for the small. Small is more important than big—that's the gospel of CI. Big successes will ensue cumulatively from a CI process. But continuous, tiny half-steps by each and every person and group are the trademark of this new game.

6. Remove the fear of failure. Speaking up and trying even tiny new things is tough enough. But living with failure in characteristically failure-adverse organizations is a much tougher nut to crack. And to be continually trying and testing the tiniest new tricks means that failures, even if they are small ones, will ensue.

7. Make recognition and celebration a CI staple. Weekly newsletters and occasional videos focusing on successes (and useful failures), spontaneous applause, weekly recognition meetings, monthly or bimonthly appreciation bashes, are a must. Use these to celebrate and record your triumphs, however small.

8. Participating in the effort must eventually become nonvoluntary. Let managers get committed at their own pace (albeit with lots of nudging and peer pressure). Early forced compliance will surely backfire. But everyone ultimately must hop on board, and those who dig in their heels too deeply and for too long must see their continuing reluctance reflected in their performance evaluations.

9. Diffuse good ideas. As CI begins to take hold, there will be lots of successes to report (and interesting failures to learn from). One person's (or team's) success can readily be copied, with appropriate adaptation and enough originality to get the copycat committed to his or her unique version of the idea. Carefully managing the good-idea diffusion process—providing lists of case data without forcing relocation—is essential to keeping up momentum.

10. Set the tone from the top—or else. If CI is not intrusive on the leader's agenda, it won't be on the agenda on the front line, where it counts. The vital issue is getting busy executives, slaves to the big picture, to lavish praise and time in support of the minuscule. Big ends will only result from small beginnings if big bosses develop an unmistakable passion for small beginnings. This is not a "pick and choose" list. Do all ten or don't bother to start. Are you game?

■ How Life Resembles Your Files

A friend once told me how a famous politician's wife—a celebrity in her own right—learned to cope with greeting the hundreds of people who regularly attended political fund-raising events at her home. She color-coded the name tag of every guest according to her level of familiarity with each person, so she would know what to say when shaking his or her hand. Contributors who had been to her home before would be given blue name tags, prompting her to say, "Hi, it's nice to see you again." First-timers would wear red tags and, consequently, would be greeted with a simple, "Hi, it's nice to meet you."

I thought this was an ingenious solution to a problem that seems to come with the territory of politics—namely, how to deal with the endless stream of people who want something from you or expect you to remember them. It followed the three basic rules of getting organized and managing your time wisely—that is, prioritizing, compartmentalizing, and maximizing.

In making a big deal out of the name tags, she prioritized; she knew that personal contact with her family was probably the reason most people came and, if managed well, would be the most vivid memory guests left with.

She also compartmentalized—by breaking down the problem into tiny increments and dealing with the one she could handle. She could have color-coded the name tags according to political leanings or pet projects or financial contributions, but she didn't. That would complicate matters. Instead, she pigeonholed people as either old-timers or first-timers.

Finally, she maximized her time. There was no wasted effort. She accomplished the task of impressing her guests in a minimal amount of time, in this case with one sentence per person. Red files, blue files.

The same method applies in business. I recently met an executive who has a color-coded solution to dealing with too much paperwork (which must be the business equivalent of the politician who meets too many people). This executive is an extremely creative entrepreneur who has had some rousing success in his career. But as often happens with risk takers, he has also gotten involved in some costly disasters.

"The big question I face every working day," he told me, "is where do I spend my time. How do I divide my energies between the good news and the bad news so that I'm dealing effectively with the money-losers but not spending so much time on them that I get depressed and forget about the money-makers?" His solution is basic prioritizing, compartmentalizing, and maximizing. He has his assistant separate all messages, letters, documents, and paperwork into two files, colored red and green. The red file is for bad news. The green file is for good news. (That's prioritizing.)

Then, he and his number two executive meet each morning to review the files. First, they go over the red file, never spending more than an hour on it. (That's compartmentalizing.) Afterward, he is free to spend the rest of the day attacking the good news in the green file. (That's maximizing.) "You can't believe what an emotional boost I get out of seeing a thin red file on my desk each morning," he says. "It's also reassuring to know that, within an hour, that red file will be sitting on someone else's desk."

■ The Danger of the Half-Baked Idea

One of our executives was heading out the door the other day for a meeting with one of our most significant clients, when a colleague grabbed him and said, "I have a great idea for your client, which you may want to bring up at your meeting." As the colleague explained his scheme with increasing enthusiasm and urgency, the executive interrupted him. "Look," he said, "if you think I'm going to my client with this half-baked idea, you're crazy. You and I know how ideas pop up and how sometimes they work out and sometimes they fall apart. But my client doesn't. He likes everything gift wrapped in a box with a ribbon around it. If I mention this project to him, and for some reason it doesn't happen, then I look foolish." Our executive was making an important point. The danger of the half-baked idea is not that it might never see the light of day, but that bringing it up, and failing to make it happen, can eat away at your credibility.

When I first started out, I realized that there were two ways I could present an idea to a client. One way was literally to tell the client everything I was working on. If there were ten projects, all unresolved but in various stages of development, I would go through them and get the client's opinion on each.

The second way was to play it close to the vest. I wouldn't mention a project until I was one hundred percent sure it was real. Only then would I present it for the client's approval. I soon realized that each approach had its own set of risks and rewards.

On the one hand, if I held off presenting an idea until it was a sure thing, there could conceivably be long periods of time when I wasn't talking to the client. The client would be left with the impression that I wasn't working very hard for him. On the other hand, if I ran to the client with every idea that popped into my head, I also ran the risk of ruining my credibility. If none of the ten projects on my plate worked out, I wouldn't blame my client for being suspicious about my competence.

Which course you choose to take in presenting your ideas (and either approach is fine) depends on whom you are dealing with. Some people can handle a wide assortment of ideas and can accept the fact that most, if not all of them, will slip though the cracks. Other people can't be bothered with half-baked ideas; they want them signed, sealed, and delivered.

■ How the Boss Sells

One of the great misconceptions of managerial life is that, at some point, the boss no longer has to sell. Not true. You never stop selling, even when you become the CEO. It's only that you sell differently. When you first start out, selling is a straightforward assignment. You ask for the order, get people to sign on the dotted line, and raise your arms in triumph when the deal is closed. There is a direct correlation between your effort and your results.

But selling becomes a little more complicated as your career progresses. Suddenly, you are managing a sales team. You pay other people to ask for the order. The correlation between your effort and your results is fuzzier because the credit for a sale isn't yours alone. You have to share it. How you adjust to this new environment can make or break a career. Here are three new sales leads for future CEOs:

1. Sell your experience. Sometimes the most valuable commodity you have to sell is your years in the business. I recently went through a hectic two-week period in which I had substantive meetings with eleven different organizations, each of which is an existing or prospective customer of ours. In not one of those meetings did I actually sell something—at least not in the customary sense of writing an order. Yet in each meeting I was selling.

2. Sell your internal strength. More than anything else, I am selling our company's bench strength. Once I've persuaded a company that they should be spending money in marketing, it's just as important to convince them that we are the most qualified organization to help them spend it.

A lot of bosses have a rough time making the ego leap from selling their talents to selling their company's strengths. It means moving the spotlight off themselves and shining it on a subordinate. And yet failing to do this is precisely why so many bosses fail at being the boss. Because once you convince people that you are the person they should be dealing with, it's only natural that they will want to deal only with you. Trying to be all things to all people, especially if you are the boss, can slow you down or bring you to a dead stop.

The easiest way to sell your company's depth is also the most obvious: Bring subordinates to meetings. Don't fly solo. The other day I brought along two key executives to a meeting with a major food service group. My presence was mostly cosmetic—to prove that we thought the relationship was important. The group identified seven areas where we could work together. As for me, I identified which person was responsible for what area. If everything works out, I won't have to spend much more time selling to this new client. Our people will do that.

3. Sell through details. I suspect not enough bosses take advantage of the fact that, being the boss, they don't have to work as hard at selling. When you're starting out, the biggest part of your job is establishing your credibility and credentials. You spend a lot of time telling strangers who you are and what you can do for them.

CEOs don't always have to go through that drill. Presumably, they already have a track record. The people they call on accept their credentials before they show up. The most effective CEOs know this, and consequently they have more effective ways of selling. In my case, that means getting the small gestures right. If selling is trying to persuade someone that they need your product or service, then I guess I'm always selling—because I'm always trying to do something to preserve a relationship or nudge it along.

In the client-management business, I'm always telling our people, "You will keep a client longer by being a very close friend and doing a not-so-brilliant job than by doing a brilliant job and not becoming their friend." This isn't a license to do bad work. It's a reminder that doing good work isn't always enough.

That's why I think my most effective brand of selling is paying attention to the personal details. If I ask about a client's family, I'm selling my concept of our relationship. If I remember what a customer likes to drink, I'm selling our company's attention to detail.

■ What to Do After "That's a Great Idea!"

An idea is never more vulnerable than in the critical moments after somebody says, "That's a great idea." This is when most people decide how they can resent the idea, how they can misuse it, lose it, neglect it, or love it to death. Here are two responses that can minimize the damage at that critical moment.

■ *Check your ego at the door.* It's easier to resent a good idea than to embrace it, especially if the creative gem is not your own. This is human nature—the not-invented-here syndrome. Many of us want to be the first to come up with a winning concept. So when we hear something really new, we get defensive. We wonder, "Why didn't I think of that?" All too often the next step is to find excuses and use self-justification to attack the idea. As an executive, you have to be aware of this all-too-human tendency ... in yourself as well as in others. Amid the excitement of the birth of a new idea, it's often hard to tell the difference between the grinding of axes and the sound of applause.

■ *Don't go by the book.* People often react to a good idea by trying to figure out what it has in common with things they've done before. They'll do this even though the product, market, timing, and people involved are completely different. The real opportunities, I've found, lie not in the similarities but the differences.

■ How to Put More Power into Your Powerful Ideas

It's one thing to come up with a brilliant idea. Making it practical and bringing it to fruition is an achievement of an entirely different order. Here are some simple strategies that will make your powerful ideas more palatable to people who are inclined to resist an idea rather than to embrace it.

■ *Hook it up to another engine.* I think so many good ideas go astray because people neglect to make them practical. It's as if they feel that their job is simply to present an idea—the more clever it is, the more "blue sky" it contains, the better—and then bask in the applause for displaying such a bold, fertile imagination. The real job of getting the idea accepted, funded, and implemented is practically an afterthought.

I try not to indulge in this ego-tripping—and I don't know many successful people who do. After all, which would you rather be, the architect whose drawing wins raves or the one whose designs get built? The easier way to add a little more horsepower to a good idea is to hook it up to someone else's engine. In our company, that almost always means tailoring an idea so that it exploits our already-existing resources.

■ *Push the good with the bad.* A good idea looks even better when it is preceded or followed by a bad one. I don't say this as an endorsement for bad ideas. But consider the following situation.

People are quite often asked to present a shopping list of ideas in a meeting. They'll have twenty ideas jotted down on a piece of paper—ideas that presumably they have given a lot of thought to. And yet it's amazing how little thought they give to the order in which they present their ideas. Most people know the obvious pattern of ranking their ideas in order of descending merit. They start off with their strongest idea and work their way down the list. The big problem with this, of course, is that your grand finale is your weakest idea!

A standup comic doesn't close his act with his weakest joke. Neither should you. Pay attention to the order in which you present your ideas—and give your audience time to digest what you are saying. If you have twenty-four ideas, no one expects all of them to be of equal brilliance. So pace yourself. Start out with a strong idea and pique everyone's interest and establish your credibility. Then go to a few marginal ideas, and then come back with a good one. And so on.

■ Why Good Employees Leave and How to Keep Them

There is no mystery to holding onto good employees:

1. Give them a lot of responsibility.

2. Don't insult them with their paychecks.

3. Tell them how they're doing.

Unfortunately, the simplicity of this approach hasn't eliminated executive turnover at most companies. Good people will always leave good firms. Here are some reasons they resign, and what you can and cannot do about it.

1. The surprise departure. It's a sign of poor management when a good employee leaves to take another job and that decision is a complete surprise to the boss. Somebody in the company should have known and made an effort to turn around the unhappy employee. The best managers are sensitive to what their people want, what motivates them, and what irritates them. Employees leave clues all over the place. They come in late, they miss deadlines, they subtly let you know that their spouse or kids hate the city they're in.

Perhaps you won't always solve what's ailing them, but you can recognize the symptoms and sympathize. Remarkably, a willing ear is sometimes enough.

2. Hating the boss. There's not enough room to go into why employees hate their bosses. But whatever is behind the conflict, the problem can usually be resolved if the boss keeps an open door. It's the manager's duty to be sensitive to his associates' ambitions. But this concern cuts both ways. Employees have to tell the boss what's bothering them. Bosses can't read minds (though they should try), but they can make it easy for employees to open up.

For myself, I will take time for anyone who asks to see me and tells me how much time he or she needs. Whether the person requires fifteen minutes or three hours, I'll be there. I have a hunch some employees don't believe me, but if they're as smart as they think they are, they will give me a try.

3. Faster than fast track. On occasion, you will be blessed with an employee who is so productive that his or her advancement through the ranks is a foregone conclusion. The question is, how far and how fast? You have to be creative in how to promote this fast-tracker, for he or she can wreak havoc with your organizational chart. If you get it wrong, you not only risk losing the whiz kid but you may offend those he or she leaves behind. Admittedly, this is a high-class headache, but don't take the situation lightly.

4. Youth with great expectations. It's a fact of corporate life that newly hired superstars, fresh out of college or business school, are the people most likely to leave you, usually within two years. They're the ones you've worked hardest to attract. They're the ones with the greatest expectations. And, sadly, they're the ones most companies neglect.

It's no surprise when smart, ambitious employees, put into entry-level positions and left to fend for themselves, soon decide to move to greener pastures. The solution: For the first twelve months, treat new hires as investments. It's expensive to lose them, because you have to reinvest in someone else. Watch the superstars when they're new. Train them. Expose them to your best people. Nudge them into projects a little beyond their experience. And as with any investment, don't expect to recoup your money right way. The payoff increases the longer the hotshots stay.

5. More money. The lure of a bigger paycheck, of course, is the main reason people leave. There's not much you can do about this phenomenon, especially if you are already paying the employee as much or more than you think he or she is worth. You can go through the ritual of making a counteroffer, but this sort of salary Russian roulette rarely pays off for the employee or the company. A study by Boydon International, a search firm, conducted among 450 executives who had recently changed jobs, found that of the forty who had received counteroffers, twenty-seven accepted the pay hike and stayed with the current employer. Within eighteen months, however, all but two had either left or been fired. Money, it seems, wasn't the solution to their problem.

■ The Ten "Demandments"

Back in the early days of the Industrial Revolution, a London factory manager compiled a list of suggestions—ten epigrammatic bits of advice that he passed along to his employees. Here are his "Ten Demandments":

1. Don't lie. It wastes my time and yours. I am sure to catch you in the end, and that is the wrong end.

2. Watch your work, not the clock. A long day's work makes a short day, and a short day's work makes a face long.

3. Give me more than I expect, and I will give you more than you expect. I can afford to increase your pay if you increase my profits.

4. You owe so much to yourself that you cannot afford to owe anybody else. Keep out of debt, or keep out of my shops.

5. Dishonesty is never an accident. Good men, like good women, never see temptation when they meet it.

6. Mind your own business, and in time you'll have a business of your own to mind.

7. Don't do anything here that hurts your self-respect. An employee who is willing to steal for me is willing to steal from me.

8. It is none of my business what you do at night, but if dissipation affects what you do the next day, and you do half as much as I demand, you'll last half as long as you'd hoped.

9. Don't tell me what I'd like to hear but what I ought to hear. I don't want a valet for my vanity but one for my money.

10. Don't kick if I kick. If you're worth correcting, you're worth keeping. I don't waste time cutting specks out of rotten apples.

■ Let's Get Rid of Management

That's what the headline of an advertisement in *The Wall Street Journal* read. "People don't want to be managed," the copy went on to explain, "they want to be led." The advertisement was by United Technologies. Writing in the December 1985 issue of *Training* magazine, John H. Zenger offers the following distinction:

Management is the administrative ordering of things—with written plans, organizational charts, annual objectives, frequent reports, position papers.

Leaders, on the other hand, provide visionary inspiration, motivation, and direction. Leadership generates an emotional connection between the leader and the led. It attracts people and inspires them to put forth incredible effort in a common cause.

We have many well-managed organizations, but few are led by great leaders. What do leaders do? Zenger offers the following behavioral dimensions:

1. Leaders create values through communication. They are great communicators. They thrive on communicating their own, and the organization's, values. Contrast this with the attitude of many managers who communicate only on a "need to know" basis.

2. Leaders develop committed followers. They meet frequently with their people to create a strong team spirit. They run effective meetings, and they understand the power of groups and the benefits of communication in a group setting.

3. Leaders inspire lofty accomplishments. They use small wins to build confidence and motivate people to do more. Then they move on to bigger challenges. Managers, in contrast, are concerned only with meeting schedules and getting results. They lack the leader's passion and commitment. They go for short-term, incremental gains, not quantum leaps forward.

4. Leaders focus attention on important issues. They use dramatic or symbolic acts to accomplish this. A company president moved his desk next to that of a troubled division's general manager to focus attention.

5. Leaders connect their group to the outside world. They serve as a link to the rest of the organization and to the rest of the world, both giving and getting information.

6. Leadership consists of observable behaviors that can be taught. Some people are born leaders, yes. But even those who are not can observe, learn, and practice to become one.

So don't stop at being a manager. Become a leader.

■ Executives Who Rely on a Very Senior Partner

"In God We Trust" is inscribed on the coin and currency we all work for. But do we trust in God? Do you? Should we pay more attention to this motto we all carry around with us?

This phrase seems to be inscribed on the minds and hearts of many of our business and political leaders. Total self-reliance is not how things actually work. For example, former Secretary of State James Baker acknowledges that in the diplomatic power game there is always a Higher Power. At the annual National Prayer Breakfast in Washington in 1991, the secretary said, "Inner security and true fulfillments come by faith. They don't come by wielding power in a town where power is king." Baker candidly stated that his wife helped him cope with a personal problem by teaching him to pray and helping him to realize his true position in life. "I really needed to stop trying to play God and turn the matter over to him," concluded Mr. Baker.

Walter Hoving, the head of Tiffany's for many years, died a few years ago at the age of ninety-one. He built sales during his tenure from $7 million to $100 million. Convinced that his entire career was guided by God, he had his jewelers produce small silver-plated pins (later expanded to include sterling, vermeil, and gold) with the message "Try God" spelled out. Was Mr. Hoving merely an eccentric business success? Is James Baker just a little unusual? I think not. The ranks of American industry and government are studded with the names of successful leaders who are not afraid to state their firm belief in God, and then, of even greater importance, to act according to that belief.

Peter Grace, formerly of W.R. Grace, has never been shy about his association with the Catholic Church and its works in the New York archdiocese. Perhaps in his environmentally sensitive business he needed all the help he could get. Tom Phillips of Raytheon, famous for its air defense systems and now making great strides in air-traffic control, started a prayer breakfast group in the mid-1980s that still meets today. Forty or more business leaders gather to discuss ethical or spiritual topics or to hear an inspirational talk at this little publicized forum.

At the worker level, small scripture-study gatherings meet at lunchtime in more and more companies. Of course, most people would rather keep their religious beliefs separate from their careers. But it's impossible to compartmentalize one's life completely. Our Constitution separates church and state, and it would be unwise to designate a company religion. On the other hand, it is difficult for any of us to deny the impact of the workings of God in the world—and that includes the business world. Worship on the weekend and business-as-usual the rest of the week isn't how things work.

Can you deny the existence of God and his workings in the world, and at the same time succeed in at least a secular monetary sense? Yes. Free will allows the world to operate in its own mysterious way. In fact, some might argue that the bottom line necessities are an occasional departure from the strict application of God's rules—an approach to which Edwin Land, founder of Polaroid, had a ready response. At one of the shareholders' meetings in 1977, Mr. Land responded to desperate reports of a product reversal. He said, "The bottom line is in heaven."

Indeed the role of providence in decisions and outcomes should not be overlooked. We are all told how important timing is in business, yet no one has any idea how to be at the right place at the right time. Some say luck is a big factor (always combined with hard work). If so, perhaps the business schools should teach a two-semester course in luck (first semester, good luck; second semester, bad luck). That curriculum would go well with a companion set of courses on timing (first semester, too soon; second semester, too late).

Many have trouble attributing specifics in business directly to God. But it is equally difficult for others to deny God's involvement. Human nature leads us to turn to God in difficult or impossible times. This phenomenon is referred to as foxhole religion in war time. There's another military saying: God is my copilot. If that's the case, why not let him take over completely? Many do. Because, after all, the higher form of human nature is to turn to God in good times.

Why do so many well-known and successful executives feel that God is a dominant force in their lives and in their businesses? The ethics of everyday operations and how people should be treated are issues that are not covered in most business schools and management texts. On the other hand, students of management commonly study the traits of successful leaders. We might do well to examine and emulate the practice of executives who rely on God. Prayer as a management technique should not be discounted.

Mr. Hoving's little pins carry a powerful message: Try God.

■ Spiritual Eldering

When we think of spiritual eldering, the paradox is that it seems like such a natural phrase. And yet in our Western culture it's not generally the way we think of growing old.

The difference between being an elder and being an old person is that an elder is somebody who has gained wisdom. Elders have distilled their life experience in such a way that their very presence becomes a witness and inspiration to others. This is what we had in early tribal society—an elder was a repository of wisdom and awareness, and younger people would check with them and say, "Am I on the right track? Am I doing right?" I like to use the word as a verb—eldering—because it is a process; it's something that we begin to grow into. Sometimes you find that the elder begins to shine forth in young children—people speak of them as having old souls.

Statistics show that many people in our culture die within two years of retirement, often because they have no goals, they have no sense of what to do with that phase of their lives.

This is where we come back to the spiritual elder. There are tools that you can use for your harvest in life, and this is how you can bring to fruition who you are and who you have become through life. Not to do so would leave our lives incomplete—like a student who has done all the work during the semester but hasn't written the exam, so he hasn't harvested the grades, the marks which demonstrate that the work has been done.

How do I save the awareness, the wisdom, the experience that I gain in a lifetime? Mostly by mentoring. When I have somebody who is eager to learn what I have to give, it releases me from grieving over my own mortality. Some day this organic, biological body will have to do what all organic substance does—get recycled. But it also contains a lot of wisdom and experience. I would grieve a lot more if that were to have to die along with the physical death. It's as if my life were a movie on old celluloid, and it's a good movie, but the film keeps ripping every time they try to project it because it's worn out. So you save it and transfer it into digital form, and now it's electronic. In a most ephemeral way it can be put into all kinds of media, and it has been saved. My sense is that it's a wonderful feeling for an elder to hand over that which he or she has gotten from life, from tradition, from generations, to the next person who can take it and put it to use.

This is something that people already in their forties and fifties need to begin to pay attention to. I can ask myself these questions: "How do I want to spend my last years? Do I want to be treated like an inmate in an institution, someone who is suddenly not capable of having his own center but who is an object for other people to store, to manipulate, to clean, to handle?" That's a very depressing thing. We have this small window of opportunity open to us, to be able to design for the up-and-coming generation an environment in which this work of spiritual eldering can be done, so that we can do this in a shared way.

—

The Penalty of Leadership

In every field of human endeavor, he that is first must perpetually live in the white light of publicity.

Whether the leadership be visited in a man or in a manufactured product, emulation and envy are ever at war—in art, in literature, in music, in industry—the reward and punishment are always the same.

The reward is widespread recognition; the punishment, fierce denial and detraction.

When a man's work becomes a standard for the whole world, it also becomes a target for the shafts of the envious few.

If his work is merely mediocre, he will be left entirely alone. If he achieves a masterpiece, it will set a million tongues a-wagging.

Jealously does not protrude its forked tongue at the artist who produces a commonplace painting. Whatsoever you write or paint or play or sing or build, no one will strive to surpass or to slander you unless your work be stamped with the seal of genius.

Long, long after a great work or good work has been done, those who are disappointed or envious continue to cry out that it cannot be done.

Spiteful voices in the domain of art were raised against our own Whistler as a Mountebank—long after the big world had acclaimed him its greatest artistic genius.

Multitudes flocked to Bayreuth to worship at the musical shrine of Wagner while the little group of those whom he had dethroned and displaced argued angrily that he was no musician at all.

The little world continued to protest that Fulton could never build a steamboat while the big world flocked to the riverbanks to see his

boat steam by.
The leader is assailed because he is a leader, and the effort to equal
him is merely added proof of that leadership.
Failing to equal or excel, the follower seeks to depreciate and to
destroy, but only confirms once more the superiority of that which
he strives to supplant.
There is nothing new in this. It is as old as the world and as old as
the human passions—envy, fear, greed, ambition, and the desire
to surpass.
And, it all avails to nothing. If the leader truly leads, he remains
the leader. Master poet, master painter, master workman—each in
his turn is assailed, and each holds his laurels through the ages.
That which is good or great makes itself known, no matter how
loud the clamor of denial. That which deserves to live—lives.

—*Cadillac Motor Car Division, advertising in* The Saturday
Evening Post, *January 1926*

■

■ Three Leadership Qualities

These three qualities are invaluable to the leader: Compassion for all creatures, material simplicity or frugality, and a sense of equality or modesty. A
compassionate person acts in behalf of everyone's right to life. Material simplicity gives one an abundance to share. A sense of equality is, paradoxically,
one's true greatness.

It is a mistake to consider a person whose only interest is self-interest
either caring or courageous. It is a mistake to rationalize that excessive
consumption contributes to the well-being of others by giving them
employment. It is a mistake to imagine that a person who acts immodest-
ly or in a superior way is, in fact, a genuinely superior person. These are
all egocentric behaviors. They isolate a person from the common ground
of existence. They produce rigidity and death. Compassion, sharing, and
equality, on the other hand, sustain life. This is because we are all one.
When I care for you, I enhance the harmonious energy of the whole. And
that is life.

■

Pearls of Wisdom

Fear is that little darkroom where negatives are developed.
—Michael Pritchard

■

I don't believe you can be in today's job with yesterday's methods and be in business tomorrow.

Ideas are a dime a dozen—but the men and women who implement them are priceless.

Vision is having an acute sense of the possible. It is seeing what others don't see. And when those with similar vision are drawn together, something extraordinary occurs.
—Shearson/Lehman Brothers

■

The difference between us and our neighbor is that we don't tell half of what we know, while he doesn't know half of what he says.
—George Prentice

■

A man who enjoys responsibility usually gets it. A man who merely likes exercising authority usually loses it.

It's easy to get good players. Gettin' them to play together, that's the hard part.
—Casey Stengel

■

What distinguishes people with high levels of personal mastery is they have developed a higher level of rapport between their normal awareness and their subconscious.
—Peter Senge

■

■ Personal Truths of Clarence Francis

You can buy a man's time; you can buy his physical presence at a given place; you can even buy a measured number of his skilled muscular motions per hour. But you cannot buy enthusiasm, you cannot buy loyalty, you cannot buy the devotion of hearts, minds, or souls. You must earn these.

The Effective Business Day

—

All men dream; but not equally ...
Those who dream by night in the dusty recesses
of their minds
Wake in the day to find that all was vanity;
But the dreamers of the day are dangerous men,
For they may act on their dream with open eyes,
And make it possible.

—T. E. Lawrence

CHAPTER 8

In recent years, an element has appeared to hasten the decision-making process, affect overall business decisions, and shed new light on "the effective business day": high technology. Word processors smother us with documents, seducing us into believing that we are adequately informed. Fax machines, e-mail, and voice mail make even the most trivial request sound urgent. Overnight deliveries force us to respond in kind. We make decisions overnight ... or even sooner.

Not long ago I was reading a history of Washington's dealings with his generals during the French and Indian War. It would take weeks or months for news of a devastating massacre of settlers to reach Washington from the frontier. Washington would rage, thump his desk, and demand vengeance. He would fire off orders—reinforcements to be mustered immediately and deployed west. But given the methods of communication in 1760, his commands moved at a pony's pace. It would take months before the men could be gathered, outfitted, and trained. By then, Washington's anger had certainly cooled and the emergency didn't seem so pressing. All of which makes me wonder if the new office technology is not prodding us to make decisions too quickly that need more thought.

How can one have an effective business day, and what does that mean? How do people work with passion? How do we find our passion? We start with ourselves. I'm often asked if everyone has passion. Yes, we all have passion within us, but few of us act on it. We buried our passion as youngsters, when we were ridiculed for getting carried away or getting too big for our britches. But those strong natural impulses still rest within. And they will resurface as we discover who we are.

The key is looking inward. To get mental clarity you must spend time with yourself. This may be awkward in the beginning. You'll find diversions, relish interruptions, write unnecessary memos. You'll feel restless—maybe even annoyed. However uncomfortable that feels, you're on the right track. The first step is the experience of clarity (or the "ah-ha"). And just before the moment of clarity comes the greatest confusion. So if you feel "stirred up," congratulate yourself. You're beginning to know yourself.

Acceptance, however, must accompany self-knowledge. To discover your passion and release your power, you must accept all of your experience as good. Powerful people do not want to be like anyone else. If you believe you are trapped—that it's only rich people, presidents of corporations, and politicians who have power—you are tyrannizing yourself.

Finding your passion is the hard part. From there, choices abound. It's a matter of being true to your newly discovered passion and building work around that. Looking for a job is very different than creating your work. Clarify what you'd like your work to be, and find a way to do it.

Passion is mandatory! There must be a fire in your belly, a passion in your gut, a sense of excitement in your sinew. You must have a missionary zeal, along with relentless pursuit of satisfying your customers, clients, and prospects.

Your passion has nothing to do with phony smiles, clever phrases, and banners with slogans. It means your ability and desire to compete profitably now and throughout the twenty-first century.

Passion is burning the midnight oil. It's going the extra mile. It's doing the unexpected. Passion is your positive attitude in a world of negativity. It's finding the extra fuel when you thought your tank was dry. It's an unwillingness to accept second best or "it's good enough." Passion somehow lets you execute even when you're exhausted. Passion pits you against your toughest competitor—you.

Passion converts suspects into prospects, prospects into customers, and customers into friends for a lifetime. Passion converts successful salespeople into superstars.

■ Some Thoughts on Starting Your Day

A friend of mine recently told me about an interesting (perhaps apocryphal) story about Henry Luce, the legendary magazine publisher and founder of *Time*. Although he was a wealthy, sophisticated businessman who could easily afford the finer things in life, Luce was notorious for his great indifference to food. He regarded the whole ceremony of dining in restaurants and entertaining business associates as a waste of time. To Luce, food was fuel, a necessary inconvenience to power him through the rest of the day.

Of course, Luce was not totally oblivious to the value of meeting people over a well-prepared meal. On one occasion he asked one of his top editors to join him for dinner at a four-star restaurant in New York. He regularly did this to trade opinions with his senior people. An elegant repast ensued. Waiters appeared and disappeared with the various courses and appropriate wines, during which Luce pontificated on the big issues of the day. As the two men finished their coffee and the table was cleared for the last time, there was a lull in the conversation. Luce looked around the room, as if searching for the maître d'. Then he turned to his editor and said, "Don't you think the service here is slow today? We've been here more than an hour and we haven't even gotten the menus yet." The meal had made absolutely no impression on Luce.

If you examined the organizational styles of most successful business people, you'd find that they all regard certain "essential" activities as extraneous. They are willing to sacrifice at least one aspect of a so-called normal business day and, thereby, use their time more efficiently.

Henry Luce eliminated the ritual of eating. Personally, I don't agree with his choice. I think you can connect with people and learn more about them over the course of a two-hour meal outside the office than you can via half a dozen meetings inside the office. But that's another story.

In a way, Luce was ahead of his time. A lot of people now treat at least one meal of the day as extraneous. Many people, I notice, sacrifice lunch to streamline their day. Some use the gained time to maintain their physique, to take care of their body. They jog or work out. Others do at lunch what I do very early in the morning—take care of paperwork, dictation, and internal matters without too many interruptions.

Likewise, the habit of getting together over drinks with colleagues after work seems to be fading. The reason: People prefer to visit a health club, take an evening class, or spend time with their family during those hours. These are commendable choices, especially if they add a little more pleasure and efficiency to your day.

I'm a little unusual when it comes to the time-consuming rituals I've sacrificed. With a lot of people, I've eliminated human pleasantries from my schedule. If a thirty-minute meeting is over in twenty-five, I don't like to fill those remaining five minutes with soft social banter as my counterpart and I struggle gracefully to take leave of one another. I end the discussion and let both of us move on to something else, which often makes me appear more abrupt than perhaps I am. This attitude is most glaring when I find myself in quasi-business situations—dealing with acquaintances rather than close friends.

I prefer the standard salutations. "How are you? Good to see you. I'll see you during the week." They are slightly abrupt, but given the situation, such common phrases get the job done, harm no one, and save me a lot of time for the people or activities that are of greater importance to me. It's a question of priorities. Do I sacrifice the small talk in order to gain an hour for myself. Or do I waste time on meaningless social pleasantries and pay for it later on? A well-organized person makes these sort of choices all day long.

Take a few minutes to examine some of the extraneous activities in your schedule. Are you spending too much time on the phone? Could you cut your conversations with customers or friends in half with no ill effect on the relationship or the bottom line?

Are you devoting unquestioned hours to paperwork that could be delegated to a subordinate or are totally unnecessary? Are you responding to memos that don't require a response? Are you calling or attending certain meetings out of habit? Would anyone notice if the meetings stopped, or if you stopped attending?

Are two-hour lunches a necessary part of your executive lifestyle? Could you accomplish just as much meeting someone over a half-hour breakfast? Would you feel better about yourself if you spent that time at the gym? Would your productivity rise or fall as a result? Why not make a promise to yourself and cut out one "essential" of the day?

Renew Your Enthusiasm

*If you can't get enthusiastic about your work, it's time to get
alarmed. Something is wrong. Compete with yourself; set your teeth
and dive into the job of breaking your own record. No one keeps up
with his or her enthusiasm automatically. Enthusiasm must be
nourished with new actions, new aspirations, new efforts, new
visions. It is a person's own fault if enthusiasm is gone; he or she
has failed to feed it. If you want to turn your hours into minutes,
renew your enthusiasm.*

—*Author unknown*

■ How to Break Away from the Pack

The first rule in setting yourself apart from the pack is to outperform the pack. The second rule is to make sure that the right people notice. Sounds simple, doesn't it? Unfortunately, it isn't.

Getting ahead has never been a simple matter of establishing your worth and then getting recognized for it. It probably should be, but most organizations are too complicated to permit that. Not only do you have to alert your superiors to your accomplishments, but at the same time you have to persuade your colleagues that it is in their best interest to support your scramble to high ground and you have to prevent them from undermining your deeds. Also, as you meet with increased success, you have to reward the peers and subordinates who backed you. You can't leave them behind. You must keep them as friends, even as they ride your coattails (and sometimes slow you down).

Setting yourself off from the crowd without giving the crowd a reason to turn on you is complicated. Here are four strategies that can simplify the effort.

1. Be visible but silent. If you're going to wage an all-out campaign to get noticed, be quiet about it. Your peers don't resent ambition (they're ambitious, too). They'd just rather not see it so nakedly displayed. Likewise, when you do achieve a modicum of visibility, downplay it. Superstar athletes, especially in team sports, know this instinctively. When running back Herschel Walker made headlines in being traded from the Dallas Cowboys to the Minnesota Vikings, he made a point of dampening the press's enthusiasm by emphasizing that he was just one of forty players. I suspect he did this not only to diminish expectations that would be impossible to live up to but because he knew his new teammates also deserved the spotlight.

2. Turn a loser into a winner. Everybody wants to play on a winner. But simply being on a winning team doesn't set you off from the pack. Nor, for that matter, does leading the winning team, especially if it has been a perennial winner. You will always be perceived as a caretaker, someone who inherited or maintained success rather than created it. You will never get the proper credit.

The key is to put yourself in a turnaround situation. At the upper reaches of the corporate pyramid, this could mean transforming an unprofitable division into a moneymaker. At the middle level, it could mean breathing new life into a moribund project. At the entry level, a "turnaround" could be something as simple but necessary as reorganizing a perennially chaotic filing system. (Someone has to do it; why not you?) Whatever your level, if you succeed where everyone else has failed, your boss will take notice and appreciate it.

3. Take intelligent risks. If you want to break out from the pack, inevitably you will have to take some risks. When the time comes, be sure your risks are smart ones. Intelligent risks are not necessarily those with a high probability of success. I think intelligent risks are those where you hedge your bets rather than plunge in recklessly, where even if you fail miserably, you haven't lost everything.

4. Change the rules. Sometimes it's easier to separate yourself from the pack by letting them run by. You stop racing and take a closer look around. I remember a young, ambitious engineer who was part of a very dynamic real estate development group. At some point, this young man realized that every engineer in his organization was as hard-working as he was. He knew he could never outdesign his peers, at least not by such a margin that he would leave them in the dust. So he changed the rules. He stopped competing as an engineer and made a lateral move into a sales position.

■ Don't Worry About What Someone Else Is Thinking About You

When you are worried about how you're coming across and are afraid you've made a blunder, remember this: You've blown it in your own eyes ... the eyes you've attributed to the other person. Your comrade doesn't see you through those projected eyes but through his or her own. Often the other person won't perceive you as blowing it at all, even when that's your evaluation of the situation. In fact, the other person doesn't even notice what you do. We're not as important to others as we think we are.

Keep alert for the next time you start worrying about what someone else is thinking about you. Now think carefully about that person. Have you been watching that person's every move with utter concentration? Have you been obsessing about how stupid his or her actions are? I'll bet the answer is no. You've been too busy with your own concerns. The same interest in self is likely true of everyone around you. Do you see the joke? Each person is too busy wondering how he or she comes across to have much time left over to pay attention to you.

Don't forget that everyone makes mistakes a million times in his or her life. That's how we learn. You don't have to—and couldn't possibly—do everything perfectly. Sometimes you trip up on one thing after another. If you're willing to laugh at yourself and shrug your shoulders, very likely others will laugh with you instead of at you. They'll throw in a little respect, too, because you are willing to accept the human condition. Actually, very few people feel camaraderie with someone who seems to do everything just right. Faced with such perfection, others feel inadequate by comparison. Most people have much more affection for someone who seems ordinary, seems to be doing the very best that he or she can, than for someone who comes on like Superman or Wonder Woman.

■ The Art of Making Decisions More Slowly

Here are three rules I've learned about making decisions.

1. Decisions made more slowly are better than those made in haste.

2. No decisions are always better than wrong decisions.

3. The world prefers decisions made quickly to those that take some time, and wrong decisions to none at all.

If you detect a conflict here, you're right. In an accelerated age, where people put a premium on speed and hyperefficiency, effective decision-making seems to be in direct conflict with how we like to use our time. I've always believed that almost any decision that can be slowed down should be slowed down, and that you have to fight like mad against the impulse to rush into a decision.

Unfortunately, a lot of people can't deal with that. They're impatient. They can't wait. For whatever reason, they need a decision now. And so they importune us for snap decisions. They make us supply answers as quickly as they ask questions. That's a dangerous way to work.

The first key in making slower decisions is accepting the fact that, quite often, nothing bad will happen if you can't or don't decide.

Doctors (and the nurses who handle their appointments) are masters at this. If you call your doctor with an urgent complaint, what happens? Chances are you don't even get through to the doctor. You talk to the doctor's nurse, who asks a few pertinent questions and then informs you that the earliest date the doctor can see you is two weeks from Monday.

"Should I schedule you for the morning of afternoon?" asks the nurse, calmly throwing the decision back to you. The nurse, in effect, is asking you, "How serious is this?" Serious enough that you are willing to make a nuisance of yourself and demand to see the doctor right away? Or can you wait two weeks, by which time the pain may have gone away?

What's wrong with this picture? In truth, nothing. Doctors know that most patients' complaints don't require immediate attention, and so they have become masters of deferring and delaying decisions until more information is available—in this case, until two weeks later, when you may be feeling much better. It's a great system for two reasons: It lets doctors address problems at their pace rather than at the pace of their patients, and it works.

The same thing happens in business. Ray Cave, who was the managing editor of *Time* magazine for nine years, once told me that he simply refused to make decisions about half the problems his staff presented him each week. That's not because Ray is indecisive. As managing editor, Ray had one of the most decision-intensive jobs in America. He faced hundreds of decisions every day. And these weren't small, self-contained choices such as whom to phone, whose calls to return, or where to have lunch. Ray's decisions had a direct impact on dozens of talented people around the world. If Ray opted to run one story rather than another, that set off a chain of consequences for a battery of reporters, writers, editors, and photographers. It also lit the fuse on a string of decisions. Once Ray knew what was going in the magazine, he also had to decide who would write it, how long it would be, what pictures to use and who would take them, and so on, for every page of the magazine, while the clock insistently ticked away toward the weekly Saturday deadline, and more and more people streamed into his office, urging him to make even more decisions.

Eventually, to preserve his judgment, sanity, and budget, Ray learned to make nondecisions. And not surprisingly, given the fact that circumstances and news events around the world changed by the hour, nearly all of the so-called pressing problems went away or popped up again as different problems. Either way, any decision would have been moot.

As Ray explains it, "If people were urging me to assign a story and I wasn't sure it was a good idea, I'd sit on it. I'd rather lose a day of reporting than have someone start on the wrong story and then have to stop and start on something else."

Another way to make decisions more slowly is to figure out why other people want you to go faster. The classic example of this is the salesperson with a quota. Salespeople always make more sales near the end of their monthly or quarterly sales cycle because they employ tactics to speed up the customer's decision—such tactics as lower prices, added incentives, and inventory clearances. In most cases, a shrewd customer would be better off deciding even more slowly—to make the salesperson more desperate and improve the terms. Most of us can sense when people are pressing us for a quick decision. But sometimes the process is very subtle; the hidden agendas are hard to detect.

■ Breakthroughs

One of the things that has become very powerful in my company is the heightened awareness that we major in breakthroughs, that we do have the technology of breakthrough. From time to time, some of us forgot the power that is available to us.

Whenever I go into an office and the level of communication between the people in that office is stories, narrative, opinion—if that's the level at which people working in that office are discussing work conditions, their intentions, their results—I know immediately that in this office there are and will be no breakthroughs. Breakthroughs don't happen at the level of opinion, narrative, or story. Breakthroughs happen as a function of vision and self-expression.

A person has to really want a breakthrough. Breakthroughs occur when people take a stand and declare themselves. Breakthroughs require being clear about what is so, rather than being entangled in a story, the explanation, or the justification. The way one turns a situation around is by getting off it. One cuts out the story, the explanations, and the justifications, and one creates the intention necessary to move one's action by making a declaration, by taking a stand.

When one comes from a sense of vision, makes a declaration, and takes a stand, then one's behavior is appropriate to the stand that has been taken. This is how breakthroughs occur.

■ Punctuality: The Hidden Persuader and the Most Underestimated Virtue

Punctuality is the most underestimated virtue in business. It doesn't require talent, money, brains, or a professional degree. It's easy to do. Nobody congratulates you for it, and if you fail, you can usually limp by with an apology. Our ready acceptance of the apology may explain why so many people are chronically late. But there are really no excuses. With so many truly tough jobs in business, we can't afford to ignore the easy ones like showing up on time.

In my experience, punctuality is the hidden persuader in every successful business relationship. Being on time is the swing vote between getting a first shot and being passed over. If you are punctual, people will not only peg you as someone who is always on time but they will also assume that you conduct all your business affairs with equal efficiency. That's a nice reputation to have, and the repercussions can be considerable.

■ *Punctuality's Payoff:* You need to establish a reputation for reliability with a sales prospect. You do that by always being on time, delivering proposals when you promise them, accurately reflecting an oral agreement in a follow-up cover letter. At some point in the future, this kind of performance will tilt the scales in your favor, even if you don't deserve it. When the next job comes up, maybe all you can offer the prospect is the assurance that you can do it. Why should he or she give you the benefit of the doubt? Because you've always delivered in the past.

I'm punctual, so I try to create split-second decisions to demonstrate my efficiency, especially with new business relationships. I will set up a phone call for ten o'clock and will call precisely as the hour tolls. I will promise to have information on a prospect's desk by Monday, and the letter will be there. I walk in the door for a 9:30 appointment at precisely 9:30. An added benefit for all of this effort, I have found, is that most people follow my lead. I start to get the same on-time response from others that they have come to expect from me ... at least most of the time.

■ How to Create an On-Time Personality

When it comes to sizing up a person's sense of time, I believe in the rule of halves. In my experience, half the world is on time, half the world is late. Half the world gets a head start on deadlines, half the world procrastinates. I can live with both halves, once I realize which half I'm dealing with. But I prefer doing business with people who are on time. I find they like to see that quality in me as well. Here are six rules that help me create an on-time personality.

1. I speed up when I'm running behind. If a thirty-minute meeting runs longer than I expected, I will cut my next meeting short to get back on track, rather than spend the rest of the day readjusting my schedule, playing catch up, or making excuses.

2. I avoid rush hours—in all their forms. That is, I do the things that everyone has to do—e.g., get to work, catch a flight, make a meeting, book a table at a popular restaurant—but I schedule these activities at times when the majority of people are least likely to do them in competition with me. This contrary attitude means I arrive at work at least half an hour before the rest of the world gets started. It means I fly at midday or in the late evening rather than fight crowds at 8 a.m. or 5 p.m. If forces beyond my control compel me to fight crowds, I follow rule 3.

3. I allow time for things to go wrong. Whether I'm going across town or across the state for a meeting, I give myself a cushion. This is an obvious precaution, yet how many people budget forty-five minutes to complete a trip that, under the best circumstances, would take sixty minutes? And then they wonder why they're fifteen minutes late (or even later)?

4. I prefer being early to being late. This is a simple matter of temperament. I know many people who regard being early for a meeting as a sign of weakness, signifying that they have nothing better to do but cool their heels in someone's reception area. Being early, I've found, not only makes a great impression but allows you time to collect your thoughts or make a few phone calls.

5. I don't let others drag me down. I thank people for being on time (so it becomes habitual) and remind them when they're not (before it becomes habitual). A manager who lets punctuality or its absence go unremarked will become a victim of time rather than its master.

6. I set my watch five minutes fast. Just for inspiration's sake.

■

Pearls of Wisdom

I have not the shadow of a doubt that any man or woman can achieve what I have, if he or she would make the same effort and cultivate the same hope and faith. What is faith worth if it is not translated into action?
—*Mohandas Gandhi*

■

The important thing is this—to be able to sacrifice what we are for what we could become.
—*Charles Dubois*

■

When you ask me what I came to do in this world, as an artist I will answer you: I came to live out loud.
—*Emile Zola*

■

Ingenuity, plus courage, plus work, equals miracles.

■

It's tough doing nothing; you never know when you're finished.

■

You will never let yourself have more money than you think you are worth.

■

■ Personal Truths of George Bernard Shaw

This is the true joy in life, the being used for a purpose recognized by yourself as a mighty one; the being a force of nature instead of a feverish, selfish little clod of ailments and grievances complaining that the world will not devote itself to making you happy.

I am of the opinion that my life belongs to the whole community, and as long as I live, it is my privilege to do for it whatever I can. I want to be thoroughly used up when I die, for the harder I work the more I live. I rejoice in life for its own sake. Life is no "brief candle" to me. It is a sort of splendid torch which I have got hold of for the moment, and I want to make it burn as brightly as possible before handing it on to future generations.

Sales and Marketing

—

One of the marketing myths is that a good idea ought to be obvious.

CHAPTER 9

There's a marketing revolution going on, and a lot of us still don't know what to do about it. We are still trying to sell hamburgers and tacos to a public clamoring for fajitas and tuna melts. Instead of listening to the consumer and trying to determine what he or she needs and wants, we're still asking how we can move more of our product out the door.

This is an era of instant gratification. You ignore the lifestyle of your customer at your peril. Department stores thought they were safe, and along came catalogs. Well, catalogs take longer to deliver their products to the consumer, said the smug store managers. Then Land's End and a lot of other catalog companies offered twenty-four-hour toll-free hotlines to take orders and overnight Federal Express service (at a premium) for those who couldn't wait a few days for UPS.

Don't tell me what you're selling. Tell me what your customer wants to buy. Don't tell me your breakfast segment is hurting. Tell me what the competition is doing to beat you. In the Southeast, McDonald's started to walk away with the breakfast business. Then along came Hardee's. Not only did it develop a sausage biscuit that was cheaper than an Egg McMuffin and just as tasty—Hardee's now has something called a Roadie, a little cardboard box in the shape of a truck that holds a sausage biscuit and a huge container of coffee, all for $1.69.

The textbooks say selling is the process of creating products and transferring them to the consumer. Marketing, on the other hand, depends on finding the needs of the consumer and filling them. The two appear to be quite similar, but in fact they are almost direct opposites. The time has come to get inside the head of your consumer and try to figure out how to satisfy his or her inner needs. If you truly understand what those are, your product or your service should sell itself.

The customer is changing more rapidly than we can calculate: telephone banking; overnight mail of even the largest packages; instant "photo-fax" transmission of letters and documents; electronic mail through modem-linked computer terminals; conference calls. These are just some of the technological developments to come along in the last few years.

Take home entertaining. What used to take several days and several sets of hands can now be accomplished by one person in a little more than an hour. Consider this: A bachelor—we'll call him Sam—decides to invite twenty friends over for dinner at his condo in Marina Del Rey, California. It's 5:30 p.m., and he's leaving his office in his Volvo turbo-diesel.

Sam goes to an ATM and withdraws one hundred dollars. Time: 5:40. He then crosses the parking lot to a Ralph's supermarket and gets a fully cooked meal of fried and barbecued chicken pieces, baked lasagna, and enough cold duck salad for twenty from the deli counter. On the way to the checkout he picks up a jug of Gallo's French Colombard wine (already chilled, of course) and passes through the express line (because he has less than fourteen items), paying $81.50. Time: 6:10. Sam then drives three blocks to his condo and sets a buffet for twenty guests. Time: 6:28. If he cares to, he can invest another ten minutes on extras, like rolling cloth napkins in napkin rings, lighting candles, and throwing around a few sprigs of ever-fresh silk flowers, providing an elegant look. He can then spend the next twenty minutes taking a shower, shaving, and changing into casual clothes. The guests were invited for 7 p.m. Sam is ready at 6:58.

The first couple arrives at 7:15. The place looks and smells wonderful. "Why Sam! What a great looking buffet. You must have been working on this all day."

Positioning, brand personality, finding the right niche for your product, your marketing strategy, and the marketing plan that grows out of it—all of these are critical pieces in constructing your life raft if you want to survive the marketing revolution.

■ When It's Too Late

A man wakes up in the morning after sleeping on an advertised bed, in advertised pajamas. He will bathe in an advertised tub, wash with advertised soap, shave with an advertised razor, have a breakfast of advertised cereal, juice, and toast (toasted in an advertised toaster), put on advertised clothes, and glance at his advertised watch. He will ride to work in an advertised car, sit at an advertised desk, smoke advertised cigarettes, and write with an advertised pen. Yet this man hesitates to advertise, saying that advertising does not pay. Finally, when his unadvertised business goes under, he will advertise that it's for sale.

The best marketing strategies usually:

- build on existing strengths

- are viewed as a decision-making process, not simply an end product

- are action-oriented

- actively involve top management

- are well communicated to those responsible for implementation.

■ Marketing Strategies That Work Harder

Today's retail environment is a jungle of product decisions for the average consumer. A typical supermarket carries more than eight thousand items; home improvement centers have between fifteen and forty thousand, depending upon their size; and discount centers have up to fifty thousand items. The decision process is further complicated by a proliferation of similar products, often with little to distinguish one from the other except their names.

Add to this situation a decline in the quantity of sales help and you have a retail environment for your product that almost discourages, rather than invites, purchasing. Certainly, advertising can help lead a customer to your product. If you have a product in a high "habit" category, need can also help drive customers to the category in a store. But at that point, only high satisfaction, a coupon, or a great price can guarantee that they will buy your brand. In a slow use-up category, with low habit and high impulse sales, you had better understand what drives that impulse and creates sporadic need.

Product categories are vastly different. Taking advantage of these differences often requires more adjustments in media buying patterns during the year. It requires a working knowledge of the retail environment. It requires a knowledge of the dynamics, volume contribution, floor environments, and needs of the retail establishments that bring customers face to face with your product.

Developing a marketing advantage also requires an understanding of today's more sophisticated consumer. Consumers are more vocal and demanding. They challenge the status quo and are not as loyal to products or services as marketers might like them to be. This is not all bad, because it means an entrenched brand can be displaced. Times and conditions are ripe for new products, innovations, and departures from the past.

■ How to Triple Your Market Through Marketing Savvy

What would you say if I could tell you how to turn 270 million Americans into 810 million—to whom you would have the opportunity to market your product/service?

And, in this coveted market, you would not have to consider changes in anything—not even per-capita spending—to permeate this consumer-driven American society.

I believe I can convince you that there is a thrice-expanded market out there, ready for your innovative ideas. These people are just waiting for creative concepts from today's marketers to capture them and work for them.

Where are the "extra" people coming from? We must count "personalities" rather than noses. As in *The Three Faces of Eve,* each of us is three different people—one person at work, another with our friends, and a third at home with our family.

These multiple personalities create multiple opportunities for marketers. When seized, these opportunities produce such sales explosions and line extensions as those recently experienced in what was simply called the tennis shoe market. There are now all kinds of specialty "sneakers"—for jogging, for basketball, and some in which to play tennis.

Over the back fence, after mowing the lawn on Saturday, the average Joe might have Becks beer with his neighbor. Come Saturday night, at the bowling alley with the team from work, he might order a Bud. And on Sunday, while watching the game on TV, he grabs a lite beer from the refrigerator.

What this says is that brand preference is determined as much by situations as by demographics. The average individual is more sensitive to what he or she may want in any environment: He or she is not less loyal—just more loyal under particular circumstances.

Complacency has no place in marketing. When you've identified your audience as to demographics, psychographics (who buys), and product benefits (why they buy), it's not time to sit back and watch what happens. It's time to evaluate the situation, or how the product is enjoyed. Appreciation for the consumer's situation can shed light on the results of a campaign. Consider: "Weekends are made for Michelob." That campaign both abdicated the work week to other beers and ignored the guzzling hour of the blue-collar worker.

The buzzword for the marketer in the nineties is *awareness*. Remain aware of every possible opportunity to triple your market by taking into consideration the "personalities" of the consumer.

■ Enough About Marketing Strategy! Let's See Some Clever Executions

The last twenty-five years have witnessed remarkable progress in management's strategic marketing sophistication. Marketing-strategy models are available that allow the manager to create a veritable strategic barnyard of cash cows, dogs, and, for all I know, birds.

Other models capture no fewer than twenty-seven of the key factors in the success of any firm's marketing moves, stir them up in a statistical stew, and fill management's plate with clear prescriptions about marketing directions.

Trouble is, strategic brilliance isn't what's lacking in a world where customers who have paid twenty thousand dollars for an automobile can't get it serviced, where corporations nominated as "key accounts" by their vendors don't know whom to call with a buying problem, and where airline travel is a string of disappointments, from the indigestible food to the surly service.

Those who do the marketing—as opposed to those who conceive, plan, and study it—are quick in their insistence that they know very well what they want to do for their customers. But they have recurrent problems getting useful things to occur in the intensely human thicket called the corporation.

If strategies often fail to work, it's usually not because the plans aren't clever enough. It's because of the new academic, consulting, and research emphasis on strategic brilliance versus tactical follow-through as the be-all, end-all of the marketing discipline.

The emphasis does far-reaching damage, not only to the poor devils who manage firms focusing so much on strategic modernity that their reason for being is sometimes forgotten, but also to the purveyors of this view, who can deceive themselves and their students into believing that marketing lies more in the planning than in the doing.

It's not even clear whether firms can be strategically differentiated any longer.

For one thing, firms within the same industries tend to engage in similar strategies because they are facing substantially the same set of environmental conditions.

The consequence is that competitive differentiation from strategic leapfrogging will help fewer and fewer firms make the kinds of returns they need in these difficult times. But managing the quality with which the strategies are executed and seeking imaginative tactics for putting plans into practice can make all the difference. Unfortunately, most firms are far better at proposing effective action than at disposing it.

■ You've Got to Do Better Than That

A leading expert on negotiation explained that there are seven magic words that drive salespeople crazy. They are, "You've got to do better than that."

The uninhibited use of this crunch technique ultimately results in false economy because the sellers soon learn to add ten percent in order to have something to shave later when the crunch comes.

Here are some tips on how to respond to the crunch technique successfully:

1. *"I understand that you want a lower price, and we will be more than happy to lower it to the level you have in mind. Let's review the options that you'd like to cut from our proposal, so we can meet your needs."*

2. *"We are building a product up to quality, not down to price. A lower price would prevent us from staying in business and serving your needs later on."*

3. *"Yes, we can do better than that if you agree to give us a larger order."*

4. *"I appreciate your sense of humor—how much better can you get than rock bottom? You see, our policy is to quote the best price first. We have built our reputation on high quality and integrity—it's the best policy."*

5. *"I'd be glad to give you the names of two customers so you can find out how much they paid for our product. You'll see it's exactly the same as we are asking you to pay. We could not develop our reputation without being fair to everyone."*

6. *"I appreciate the opportunity to do a better selling job. Obviously, you must have a reason for looking exclusively on the dollar side of our proposal. Let's review the value you'll be receiving."*

■ Baseball and Marketing Have a Lot in Common

Play ball! Baseball and marketing—could there be a connection? Both rely on personal ambition, drive, self-awareness, and attitude. It's that extra effort that brings the little victories that add up to the major successes, winning seasons, and World Series victories.

In baseball, know your strengths. Play within yourself, but always try to improve.

In marketing, know what it takes to win, and develop your skills accordingly. Hire top people to help you compensate for your weaknesses.

In baseball, you get instant feedback. One, two, three strikes, you're out.

In marketing, set goals, push yourself, keep your expectations of yourself high, and review your accomplishments.

In baseball, dig in, step out, let 'em know it's your turf. Look relaxed, stare down the opponent, anticipate your competitor's best, and try to make it happen. Remember, you get three chances.

In marketing, be confident, not arrogant. Project a positive self-image. Let people know you're there. Be a good, ethical competitor. A good winner and a good loser. But take control; do something.

In baseball, the great hitters visualize the ball sailing over the fence. Their muscles are tuned to physically re-create that mental picture.

In marketing, take time to "think." Visualize closing that sales presentation, that award-winning commercial—then make it happen.

In baseball, success requires dedication—and usually fame, fortune, and a trade.

In marketing, dedicate yourself to excellence. It will probably require a shift in personal priorities. Expect to move around a little. Get that experience with other "clubs," especially as you start out.

■ Ten Truths You Must Never Forget About Marketing

1. The market is constantly changing. New families, new prospects, new lifestyles change the marketplace. Nearly one-quarter of the people in America will move this year. Nearly five million Americans will get married. When you stop advertising, you miss evolving opportunities and stop being part of the process. You are not in the game.

2. People forget fast. Remember, people are bombarded with thousands of messages daily. An experiment proved the need for constancy in marketing. Advertising was run once a week for thirteen weeks. After that period, sixty-three percent of the people surveyed remembered the advertising. One month later, thirty-two percent recalled it. Two weeks after that, twenty-one percent remembered it. That means seventy-nine percent forgot it six weeks after the last advertising message.

3. Your competition isn't quitting. People will spend money to make purchases, but if you don't make them aware that you are selling something, they'll spend their money elsewhere.

4. Marketing strengthens your identity. When you quit marketing, you short-change your reputation, reliability, and the confidence people have in you. When economic conditions turn sour, smart companies continue to advertise. The bond of communication is too precious to break capriciously.

5. Marketing is essential to survival and growth. With very few exceptions, people won't know you're there if you don't get the word out. And when you cease marketing, you're on the path to nonexistence. Just as you can't start a business without marketing, you can't maintain one without it.

6. Marketing enables you to hold onto your old customers. Many enterprises survive on repeat and referral business. Old customers are the key to both. When old customers don't hear from you or about you, they tend to forget you.

7. Marketing maintains morale. Your own morale is improved when you see your marketing at work. Your employees' morale is similarly uplifted. Cutting out marketing seems to be a signal of failure to those who actively follow your advertising.

8. Marketing gives you an advantage over competitors who have ceased marketing. A troubled economy can be a superb advantage to a marketing-minded entrepreneur. It forces some competitors to stop marketing—giving you a chance to pull ahead and attract some of their customers.

9. Marketing allows your business to continue operating. You still have some overhead: telephone bills, Yellow Pages ads, rent and/or equipment costs, possibly a payroll, your time. Marketing creates the business that pays for the overhead.

10. *You have invested money that you stand to lose.* If you quit marketing, all of the money you spent for ads, commercials, and advertising time and space becomes lost as the consumer awareness it purchased slowly dwindles away. Sure, you can buy it again. But you'll have to start from scratch. Unless you are planning to go out of business, it is rarely a good idea to cease marketing completely.

■ Marketing with Integrity

Is the phrase "marketing with integrity" really an oxymoron? If we're referring to traditional marketing, especially as practiced by many within the food service and hospitality industries, the answer is undoubtedly yes. In perception and in action, marketing too often relies essentially on commotion, excitement, agitation. In my view, that's simply because it takes an enormous amount of energy to move something that's stuck. This all adds up to wasted motion, something we cannot afford in a business that takes up vast amounts of energy even in its simplest formats.

But marketing with integrity is more than an alternative way to do business. It means taking a whole new approach to doing business. It means integrating a way of life and the way of business. It means introducing authenticity into the process from the outset.

Marketing with integrity does not have to be an oxymoron. Authenticity is possible. According to the dictionary, the word *authentic* is synonymous with *real* and *genuine*. But when I cite authenticity and integrity here, I am dealing in human terms.

To me, Spencer Tracy was authentic. So were John Wayne and Katharine Hepburn. Their personalities infused their screen personas. Their own character, whether or not you liked it, was one and the same as the roles they played. Of course, most people did like them ... whether Tracy played a fisherman or a judge, Wayne a cowpoke or a Marine, Hepburn a young athlete or an aging woman. (Yes, there are newer stars, but my trio underscores the endurance of integrity.)

This type of enduring integrity is what you are looking for in marketing, and obviously, it has to begin at the heart of your organization. Your employees are the very first group you want to adopt the concept of integrity and adapt to its standards.

For a moment, I thought of saying that you want your employees to "buy into" the concept of integrity. But "buying in" suggests a commercial transaction, and that's the kind of attitude that we are trying to step beyond. Using this type of business language is precisely what makes people and their contributions seem very unimportant, and it keeps work from being a truly fulfilling activity.

We need to move from transactional stances to relationships. And this requires a substantive shift in the way we are used to doing things with our employees. It means moving from control to trust, replacing external coercion (salary, promotion, tenure) with a shared conviction that motivates the entire organization.

The risk here is that your employees may come to realize that what you are offering them is not really appropriate for who they are willing to become. But those who don't share your vision sufficiently to achieve fulfillment should leave your organization. It will be better for them, and it will give you an organization that speaks strongly and with a concerted voice.

At this point, you may be wondering if I'm writing about marketing or a personal philosophy. The answer is that I am writing about both, about bringing yourself to your business and applying that self to making the business work. Yes, it might require change to create this integrity, but it is a change that you will find comfortable as well as challenging.

What you need to instill in your employees and yourself is the ability to recognize opportunity, and once you've recognized it, the ability to pursue it without being confined by self-limiting or contradictory beliefs.

Once you've accomplished these organizational goals, you'll be ready to externalize them, to turn from transactions with customers to relationships with them. You'll find that customers are actually eager for these relationships, eager to be valued as human beings, eager to have their intelligence respected, eager to be regarded as more than sources of revenue.

Once you match the belief in your own services and products with the consumer's eagerness to be treated with respect, you'll find that you've entered a different, higher plane of marketing. You'll have realized what few marketers ever do: how desperate the need to belong and to be embraced is among the public.

This goes back to the tragic irony in our society that with so many people around us, we are often deprived of intimate affiliations and are very sensitive to any kind of separation or alienation. It's easy for us to forget, on the surface at least, that up until the second half of this century, most people in this country were born, lived, died, and were buried all within a few blocks or miles. They lived in families and clans within tiny villages. They knew just about every other person with whom they came in contact, and they knew them well.

Consider how different our society is today. Geographic and social mobility constantly tear us away from family and friends. We end up scattered across the country and then find ourselves thrown into huge crowds of total strangers. In this environment, it is no wonder consumers react favorably to approaches appealing to warmth, to connections. Just read the following connective advertising lines and see how quickly the name of the company comes to mind:

Fly the friendly skies ...
Reach out and touch someone ...
When you care enough to send the very best ...
Nothin' says lovin' like something from the oven ...

Then, let's look at the goods and services purchased because they seem to provide the craved-for sense of belonging. These include clothes, watches, luggage, and sports equipment that bear special insignia identifying the wearers or users with a special class of people.

In this context you must realize that today's consumers have:

1) an almost insatiable need for friendship and respect

2) a diminishing number of traditional sources for affiliation

3) a willingness to use their resources for commercial relationships that promise affiliation.

No, you can't normally provide services and products that really fulfill deep human needs. That is something only other humans can do. But you can treat people humanely and have them react to you positively. In industries like hospitality and food service, which promote or enhance human interaction, the opportunity for such positive reaction is especially attainable.

People have been bombarded with intelligence-insulting lies so often and for so long, truth has become a novelty. Experts note that the junk ads resulting from this consumer/insolence technique have given the edge to the honest, no-nonsense marketer. As Paul Hasken commented in *Growing a Business,* "Honest copy and ads come across as a refreshing change; we immediately recognize the authenticity and are disarmed."

So marketing with integrity is building relationships with customers—not simply as a better way to get them to purchase your services and products, but because you value them as human beings. It means respecting their intelligence, communicating clearly who you are and what you offer, and trusting that the right people will be drawn to you and your offerings.

But remember, you can only reach this goal if you start the process internally, changing the focus of your entire organization, even risking having to replace people within that organization. Marketing with integrity is a start-to-finish concept. It is a concept that will allow you to approach your customers as human beings, recognizing their wants and their need to belong. This will allow you the opportunity to fulfill their needs while fulfilling your own.

■ How to Be Number One Without Being Number One

Your business can be number one! Does that statement sound extravagant to you? It shouldn't. But if it does, it's probably because you're not focused on what being number one really means, and that could signal that you're not getting all you can and should from your business.

Let's start with what constitutes being number one. To some, being number one means being the biggest. Others think that being the most profitable makes them number one. Neither is necessarily right.

This leads us to Peter Drucker's observation that a business must be the right size for its market, its economy, and its technology—and the right size is whatever produces the optimal yield from the firm's resources.

We're not talking theory here but reality. If you focus on this reality, you can take on the most formidable competitors and win. You just have to learn that you don't do it head on and you don't do it all at once.

You have to remember that the big adversary can be so busy defending his or her entire position that he or she won't or can't lower his or her sights or status to what he or she views as a minor skirmish. That attitude gives you an opportunity to dominate in your own territory, even if it is relatively small. In that territory, you can be number one.

In marketing circles, this approach is sometimes called niche marketing. The trick is to find a niche for your operations in which you simply are better than anybody else—and exploit that position to maximize growth.

It may be that you've already done this, so you know that this kind of domination and growth requires concentration—mental concentration and concentration of your efforts. The greatest mistake in undertaking a growth strategy—and the most common one—is to try to grow in too many areas. Again, according to Drucker, a growth strategy has to think through the targets of opportunity—that is, the areas in which your company's strengths are most likely to produce extraordinary results.

Where can you find your niche? I believe that there are four ways in which you can differentiate yourself from the competition. And remember, the greater your differentiation, the greater your chances for success. Of course, I'm talking about meaningful differentiation, not just a rehash of some "me too" ideas.

First, pick a certain type of consumer and set out to make that type of consumer a fanatic about your operation—someone for whom your operation sets off not only bells and whistles but the cannons from the *1812 Overture*. For example, the coffee business is dominated by brands like Maxwell House and Folgers; but there is a group of competitors who have built very healthy and profitable businesses in the coffee category. One of these smaller—but vigorous—competitors is Kava coffee. This firm recognized the existence of a sizable group of coffee drinkers who love the brew but hate the acidity. Kava has said, in effect, we can't attack Maxwell House or Folgers head on, but we can carve out a niche share of the market by appealing to people who suffer because of the acidity. So, Kava appeals to one specific group of coffee drinkers and to that group, Kava is number one. You must ask—and answer—the question: What consumer can I serve as number one?

The second step has to do with producing the "special kind of experience" the consumer gets when he or she visits your establishment. Now, I wouldn't presume in this abbreviated space to tell you what kind of special experience you could give your fans. That's got to emanate from your own expertise and knowledge of what you can provide that is different and distinctive in service or product or a combination of them both. What I can tell you is: Don't hide your differentiation. You've got to go public to gain and maintain your singular niche. Even though this seems like an obvious caution, you'd be truly surprised at how many firms defer or underdo the advertising or promotion it takes to bring their niche to fulfillment.

The third niche opportunity has to do with the penetration of new units, filling in the gaps on a calculated but accelerated basis. You can do this by cultivating stronger relationships with your operators/managers, so they keep you informed about new opportunities.

New market penetration requires constant monitoring. It's not simply a case of sporadically checking with your local operators or managers. You should do so on a regular, planned basis. This requires strong relations with your operator community; the members of that community can alert you to real opportunities to profit from expanding the exploitation of your niche. Just don't leave this to chance.

The fourth route to successful niche marketing is price or added value. A warning here is that price cannot mean continuing heavy discounting to undersell the competition. No one can have the lowest price all the time. But you can give added value for price constancy.

Price and added value must be sold—just as you differentiate your product or service. As I said, no one can undersell the competition all the time. So you must build and enlarge the perception that what you offer the customer is worth what will be paid for it, if not more!

So, the opportunity to be number one in a territory that you select is up to you. You can be number one with courage, foresight, and the determination to create, and sell to, your own niche.

■ The 35 Principles of Underdog Marketing

Throughout history, time and again, the underdog has snatched victory from the jaws of defeat. In Biblical times, the bookies made Goliath an odds-on favorite over David, but you know how that contest turned out. From Truman's upset of Dewey in 1948 to the Outback Steakhouse victory over the big, casual theme restaurants that stunned the food-service world, underdogs have been turning preconceived notions upside down. But the winning performances of these underdogs were not flukes. Their victories were the result of careful preparation. Truman's campaign was a snapshot of neighborhood marketing—by train he carried his message from neighborhood to neighborhood and town to town, winning more and more voters along the way. While Dewey got all the headlines, including the famous and fateful banner that falsely proclaimed him the victor, Truman won the White House—dramatic proof that those who conduct the big media campaigns don't always emerge victorious.

Outback Restaurants orchestrated their win over the competition by building an indomitable force from within their four walls. Every merchandising zone inside the restaurant became a potent marketing weapon loaded with points of persuasion. In a stroke of strategic genius, Outback gave each of its general managers equity ownership in their own stores, generating an esprit de corps that turned Outback's internal customers into fierce warriors whose only mission was to vanquish their foes by dazzling their guests. People thought it was "just another steakhouse," with no guarantee of victory. But the owners of Outback knew what nobody else knew—that they would win. They saw the fire in the eyes of their warriors long before the competition did.

Underdog marketers are marketing warriors. They fight for high adventure, for sublime wisdom, for sound strategic thinking and exceptional brilliance. Real confidence does not come from affirmations, visualizations, mantras, a thirty-second walk on hot coals, or an Armani suit and a slick direct-mail piece. "Mustard on your Sword" confidence comes from knowing exactly how to create target-market dominance. Forget market share—crush, conquer, and befuddle the competition. Because as they say in the South, "if you ain't the lead dog, the view never changes."

Whenever the battle seems lost, whenever the war seems hopeless, underdog marketers can refer back to the following thirty-five basic principles that will provide the guiding philosophy to their cause and the reasons they will ultimately succeed. While many of these principles are specific to the restaurant industry, all can be applied with some modification to businesses of any type.

1. It's not the size of the dog in the fight that matters, it's the size of the fight in the dog. If the underdogs want to run with the big dogs, they must get off the porch and have the discipline to prepare. Underdogs are scrappy, untiring fighters for their cause. They bounce back from nips and bites to attack bigger dogs again and gain. Feisty and independent by nature, they know they might make up for their smaller size by becoming fiercely aggressive and highly disciplined, especially when defending their home territory.

2. Underdog marketers look, act, and feel like leaders. They cast a larger-than-life shadow across the path of the nearest big dogs and watch them shrink. If the underdog can project the image of the big dog and bark as loud as he does, before you know it, everyone will be pointing to the underdog as the big dog, instead of the other way around. Underdog marketers never expect a pit bull idea to be embraced by a toy poodle mind.

3. Underdog marketers are Olympic thinkers who settle for nothing less than gold medal results. The underdog marketers will not accept second-place finishes. They perform to the maximum and refuse to even consider the possibility of failure. Olympians and underdog marketers do not make excuses. They know that a good excuse for poor performance is no substitute for success.

4. Underdog marketers don't mourn the death of mass marketing, they celebrate it. Underdog marketers pronounced mass marketing dead long before the competition realized it was ailing. The underdog knows the battlefield has changed and the conventional weapons of misguided and antiquated media campaigns are the equivalent of the rusted cannon balls sitting in front of a town hall. While the competition continues to shell the market with everything in the Madison Avenue arsenal, the underdog marketers have focused their battle plans—they are conquering their own neighborhoods and winning the war.

5. Underdog marketers know that the power of persuasion begins in their places of business. Realizing that their restaurant is the most powerful selling tool of all, the underdogs use every inch of their property to carry the important messages to the thousands of customers who flock through their doors. From the valet in the parking lot, to the exterior signs, to the four walls, the underdog marketers divide the restaurant into persuasive merchandising zones. They never miss an opportunity to tell the guests what makes their restaurant special.

6. Underdog marketers use their forces wisely. They have the wisdom to fight the battle where they can best win the war—inside their four walls and in their own neighborhoods. The underdogs know that there are only four ways for sales increases to explode the top line: 1) by bringing in new customers, 2) by attracting more repeat patrons, 3) by raising check averages, and 4) by increasing party size. These sales targets are the focal point for the underdog's prime marketing objectives.

7. Underdogs know that what's right at home is best. Underdogs spend at least sixty percent of their marketing dollars right at home—within the four walls of their restaurant. The underdog marketers take control of their four walls and their message centers or zones to create messages that zero in on the minds of their best customers. Underdog marketers know what to say, when to say it, and best of all, how to say it. This turns the zones into point-of-persuasion money machines. The underdogs do not have to begin comparing drive time and weekend-insert costs before announcing that their burgers have twelve different cheese toppings. Their message centers—table promotions, tentcards, posters, and menus—will advertise that they offer everything from Gorgonzola to Monterey Jack to keep cheeseburger fanatics in their camp.

8. Underdogs use "trickle-down marketing" in reverse. Underdog marketers know how quick and easy it is for the entrepreneur to put a new idea to work, compared with big brass marketers who must start with big ideas that cost big bucks—then rush to justify the expense. Working from the bottom up, the underdogs expand their marketing effort by taking small steps first, then lengthening their stride until they are at full speed to accomplish the objectives. Meanwhile, the big dogs continue to develop their strategies while gazing downward from Mount Olympus, hopelessly out of touch with the local marketplace.

9. Underdogs may not bark the loudest, but they bark more often. Their audiences are specifically targeted, so they have more personalized communication with consumers than the big dogs' broad-based messages.

10. Underdogs conceptualize their battle plan. Whenever they think of a new promotion, menu item, or service, they realize the value of their own property first. Underdog marketers put their advantages to work by devising an overall marketing strategy that starts within the zones of their own four walls and property line before extending themselves into the neighborhood.

11. Underdog marketers know "four walls" marketing begins with the people who share their foxholes. The underdog marketers' programs don't start with a thousand fliers in Kmart's parking lot, they begin with their employees. The underdog marketers energize their staff by keeping them focused on what strategies will keep customers returning and what can be done to explore potential new business. Underdog marketers let customers on both sides of the kitchen door tell them what they think. In return, these internal customers reward the underdog marketer with their loyalty.

12. Underdog marketers know there is a secret revolution going on. Expensive advertising and sales campaigns dazzle and distract, but underdog marketers quietly sneak up on their competitors. Without fanfare, they identify the best prospects and customers by name and address—and gain their deep loyalty. Building a highly loyal customer base is an integral component of the underdog's basic business strategy. The underdogs know that a database of loyal customers is the most critical part of the marketing arsenal. They know that building relationships on a one-to-one basis with their customers will make them their first choice when they decide where to spend their food dollars. It's much easier—and less costly—to bring in current customers ten percent more often than it is to increase new visits by ten percent. This kind of marketing almost never gets the big headlines that the latest costly image campaign does. Why? Because editors and publishers still think in terms of the big media campaign. A sixty-million-dollar TV campaign is treated as far bigger news than the development of a customer club with fifty-thousand members—even though the latter may have a much more profound effect on share of market.

13. Underdog marketers know that their ability to sustain a large base of loyal customers is a powerful key to the success of their business. They know that loyal customers are the marketing apostles who spread the good word about their restaurant. The underdog marketers understand that a five-percent increase in customer loyalty can produce double-digit profit increases. They realize that word of mouth, the most effective kind of advertising, can generate exponential numbers of potential customers for their business.

14. Big dogs with deep pockets can generally win a war of attrition. Unless the underdogs can sell what the big dog sells for less, they should not challenge the big dog to a price war. That only puts the fight on the big dog's terms. Even the most persistent underdogs know that they cannot match big dog bankrolls. So to put the odds in their favor, they keep backyard battles manageable. The big dog's standardized price structure provides a foundation from which a service-savvy or quality-conscious underdog marketer can charge a premium. The underdog marketer's best effort will always outstrip the big dogs—who are tied down by limitations and procedures dictated by chain-wide red tape. Unlike the big dogs, underdog marketers are free to take their best shot whenever it serves their best interest. The underdog knows that failure is not an option—it's just a nagging possibility that keeps him focused.

15. Practice "corporate judo" when challenging a leader. Underdogs think smart (and get the most for their buck) by outmaneuvering the big dogs in every way they can, from promotional events to the purchase of product lines. If the big dog offers a beverage with his superburger, the underdog should give away free refills. If the big dog offers a coupon for twenty-five cents, the underdog should make his fifty cents. If the big dog offers free dessert for birthdays, the underdog should offer a free meal. Always embarrass the big dog by turning his own weight and size against him; then outdeliver him with product excellence and friendly service he cannot hope to match.

16. An underdog counteroffensive is doubly offensive to big dogs. The big dog's brass does not want to become increasingly involved with the underdog's counteroffensive tactics, but these tactics will win the underdog many allies. The public loves a good fight. If a company is properly branded, the underdog, the public and the media are more likely to take its side. Everyone loves the underdog.

17. Underdog marketers make innovation, service, pricing, or quality their strongest attribute. Once the underdogs make their choices, they stake their reputations on them. They never pass up the opportunity to tell the public why they are the very best there is in their distinguishing area. The underdogs know there is no reason to exercise stealth in the heat of battle. Once the all-out battle has begun, they press the initiative to the limit of their capabilities and then attack again.

18. Getting your share of stomach means elevating products and service over the big dog. Underdog marketers demonstrate why they are aware of the areas in which they excel: quality of product, service, and know-how. They get on top because big dogs seem to sleep a lot and miss much, and haven't yet figured out how to motivate their staff to match the loyalty the underdog commands among his internal customers. It's the point upon which a battle often turns.

19. Underdog marketers create a distinctive personality. They are youthful, hip, even a bit irreverent. They bark a lot and keep clamoring for attention. Brash personalities are always more engaging and memorable than those that exist inside corporate boardrooms. A bright and energetic attitude is what the public expects but so often fails to find in the typical chain operation, with its crafted duplications. The underdogs create a *unique selling proposition* (USP) that distinguishes them from their competitors. The USP becomes the badge the underdogs place on all of their marketing messages. What makes the underdog's product a unique selling proposition may be lower price, higher quality, better service, customization, ease of purchase, and ideally, a combination of these things. The USP assures that underdog marketers practice human marketing—they become the preferred supplier of what they sell. The USP tells the underdog's customers—and the world—why the underdog is the only oyster in the sea for them.

> The plainest oyster in the Dismal Sea
> Said she'd open her heart, but only for me,
> And while billions of oysters there may be,
> No one will ever taste as delectable as thee.

20. Underdog marketers practice transcendental marketing. They know that human desire transcends time, language, and culture. Since the beginning of time, people have desired health, happiness, status, security, beauty, and prosperity. In Indiana, security might be a hundred thousand dollars in the bank. In Macedonia it could mean having a government job for thirty years. And in Beirut it might mean having an assault rifle nearby. The specifics of these desired qualities may change in different areas and times, but the basic desires transcend all. Underdog marketers make sure all their marketing speaks to these basic human desires.

21. The underdog marketer creates "Eye-full Towers." The underdogs place wine bottles on their tables and prepare dessert carts that are brimming with sweet temptations. They exhibit all their products in the most dazzling and spectacular ways to entice their guests. The underdog marketer knows: "What the eye admires, the heart desires."

22. Underdog marketers know where to set their traps. Underdogs take the long-range view of building a large customer base from within.

Serving 125 customers at $6 each is better than getting 75 customers to spend $10 each. The underdog marketer knows that it is better to insulate with volume than to lose major revenues if customers drop off. Underdog marketers can always build better averages once the customer base is solidified.

23. Underdog marketers know the marginal net worth of a customer. If underdog marketers determine that a new customer represents a thousand dollars a year in profit, and they can attract that new customer through a marketing program that costs only a hundred dollars, they jump at the chance to take advantage of this tenfold return on their investment. The underdog marketer also knows that if he teaches his staff to become marketers instead of order-takers, he can add a buck to the check of every new customer without having to spend a dime in advertising costs. These are the most basic, commonsense laws of marketing, and the ones that are the most overlooked.

24. Underdog marketers know that all marketing efforts must lead with the benefits, then substantiate with the features. Consumers buy what they need when they're reminded of what they need. For example, some key benefits of a Burger King Whopper are: It's cheap, it's close to where you are, and you can almost always get it without waiting. A strong feature of the Whopper that substantiates its benefits and reminds customers of what they need from the product is that, just as Burger King's slogan proclaims, you can "have it your way."

25. Underdog marketers tell the whole story and educate their prospects about all the reasons they should be buying from them. Underdog marketers know that informed customers make educated purchases. When a customer knows everything he needs to know about the underdog's products, he'll buy with confidence, knowing that he's made the right choice. Underdog marketers know that products aren't sold—products and services are bought.

26. Underdog marketers don't depend on the grand slam or the Hail Mary pass. They know that more ball games are won on timely singles and doubles than grand slams. They practice continuous innovation in every aspect of their business and do so in small, carefully planned plays, or increments, to ensure maximum effectiveness. Underdog marketers know that counting on the big bang to make big bucks is like finding a twenty-dollar bill on the street: You're glad you've found it, and of course you'll use it, but you wouldn't head to the supermarket expecting to find twenty dollars on the way to pay for the groceries.

27. Underdog marketers know that promotions tickle the funny bone, gain consumer interest, and convince them that they want to spend time in a relationship with a brand. Underdog marketers know that promotion is the art side of marketing. The logical side is pricing strategy, product, menu, operations, and customer service. The art side of marketing says, "Who would have thunk it?" when a promotion strikes a chord among the target audience.

28. Underdog marketers know that promotion and advertising are very fashion-driven and ask consumers to "badge" with their brand. The term comes from the beer industry, where consumers identify themselves by the brand of beer they drink, by the badge on the label. When underdogs promote, they want the customer to badge to their brand or the activity that the underdog marketers are co-branding. A great promotion is a relationship—a way to say, "Spend a few minutes with me and have a little fun."

29. Underdog marketers know their traffic generators. Underdogs make a special effort to involve other nearby retailers in the trading area, including those in a shopping center across the street, as valued customers and customer contacts. Generators exist on every main street or side street in the underdogs' neighborhoods—in the schools, neighborhoods, hotels and motels, retail stores, and commercial and industrial complexes. The smart underdog marketers regularly involve those traffic generators in promotional efforts.

30. Underdog marketers use technology as a tactic. They tilt the playing field in their favor by being the first to adapt technological strides that are obviously going to become industrywide. Big dogs necessarily wade through layers of corporate paper, home-office bureaucracy, and territoriality before implementing change. The quicker the underdogs move, the slower big dogs appear to be moving.

31. Underdog marketers know when it's best to be a settler rather than a pioneer. The underdog marketers aren't afraid to blaze new trails, but they pick their ventures in innovation carefully. They don't forge trails that might lead to more peril than profit. For example, with the explosion of new technology, rather than building an elaborate web site, the underdog marketer waits for a report on the subject before making a decision.

32. Underdog marketers know that prescription before diagnosis is malpractice. When an ailing business needs major surgery, underdog marketers are smart enough to use more than a Band-Aid. While the big dog's marketers try various remedies, hoping that one of them works, the underdog prescribes the right medicine based on careful testing, insightful research, and thorough knowledge of the market conditions. Underdogs get rich by dominating their niche. The underdogs don't have the firepower to stand toe-to-toe with the big dog in every battle. They use their ammunition wisely by finding a niche in the market that they can claim as their own, and they exploit that position to maximize growth. They are the top dogs in their specialty because they offer the best product, value, and service. And any big dog that dares to invade the underdog's niche will suffer the consequences.

33. The most successful underdogs plan for war by conducting thorough reconnaissance. The wise underdog warriors know that it's futile and foolhardy to launch an attack without carefully gathering intelligence about their targeted customers and their own front-line forces (internal customers). They also know that they must accurately map the battlefield where the fighting will occur in order to conquer the enemy. They use Customer Attitude Profile Surveys (CAPS) to discover the attitudes and purchase patterns of the consumers they are targeting, and Internal Customer Surveys (ICS) to measure the battle-readiness of their staff. Underdog marketers never go to war without determining the boundaries and size of their trading area. They learn the lay of the land by conducting Trading Area Tracking Surveys (TATS), which empower them to focus and effectively target their marketing efforts in those areas most likely to generate business.

34. Underdog marketers distance themselves from the competition by measuring what they manage. Underdog marketers know their successes cannot be validated, performance cannot be evaluated, and rewards cannot be given objectively without reliable forms of measurement. In addition, underdog marketers realize that, unless rewards are connected to success, there is no motivation to achieve excellence. The underdog marketer knows you cannot manage success unless you can measure it.

35. Underdog marketers operate every aspect of their business from a marketing perspective. The successful Underdog marketer knows that a 2-percent increase in sales is better than a 10-percent reduction in expenses. The Big Dog doesn't realize that the time when he could operate himself to a profit has passed. Meanwhile, the Underdog focuses on building top-line sales to create room for the business to grow comfortably without having to gasp for air every time the climate changes.

■ How to Be a Trendsetter

Marketers who want to be trendsetters can't afford to play it safe and wait for obvious trends to develop. They have to be able to spot trends before they become visible to competitors.

How? By learning how to employ "pattern recognition"—a way of observing individual changes in society and seeing them as parts of a pattern that offers new market opportunities. Some suggestions:

■ Be alert to what's happening in totally unrelated fields. Don't get trapped in your own narrow category of interest. Read and observe widely.

■ Avoid being detail-oriented. Look for basic patterns. Specific expressions of what may be a basic pattern might not represent long-term opportunities.

■ When you find changes occurring, ask why. Examples: Why are certain occupational groups growing? Why has foreign competition become so prominent? Why is ethnic food consumption on the increase?

■ Don't depend on a single source when you accumulate data. Look for converging evidence that supports the basic pattern you have observed.

■ Ten Great Myths of Marketing

The term *marketing* came into widespread use in business during the seventies. Although major companies have long had sophisticated marketing departments, only recently has the average businessperson been aware of the value of marketing. Today, we hear business leaders talking about their firms being marketing-driven. In effect, marketing—the process of getting and keeping customers—provides the direction and growth for companies large and small.

Yet even among some of the more enlightened business leaders, there remains confusion, misunderstanding, and downright ignorance when it comes to fully appreciating the power of marketing in today's constantly changing economy. The following catalog of ten of the most common marketing misconceptions presents clearer direction for companies that want to engage in a successful and cost-effective marketing program.

1. Our salespeople are our marketing team. On the surface, this comment would seem to make sense. But it expresses a total misunderstanding of the separate roles of sales and marketing. The role of marketing is not to make sales. It is to create the right conditions so that more sales can be made. In some cases, it is to give support so that a sales force can be more effective. Other times, it is to provide leads. Certainly it is to create a preexisting climate so that prospective customers will want to do business with you.

2. We already know who our customers are. The implication here is that the company has totally identified its market. It is also an indication of incredible smugness and stagnation. One of the chief functions of an effective marketing program is the continual cultivation of existing customers.

In today's competitive environment, the process should be constant and intense. Whether or not you know where your customers are, some thought should be given to the unavoidable fact that your competition is likely to know where they are. Unless you work to keep those clients, it could be bye-bye time.

3. The only important thing to the customer is price. This always sounds so hard-hitting and businesslike. It is actually little more than total nonsense. A recent study of business-to-business purchasing showed that only six percent of all purchases are based strictly on price. Anyone trying to build or sustain a business on price alone won't be around long. One of the essential goals of effective marketing is to create a climate in which people will want to do business with you. When that happens, price alone will be way down on their list of concerns.

4. Advertising is just a waste of money. The first major error in this statement is that it equates marketing with advertising. An effective marketing program includes three goal-oriented elements aimed at meeting specific objectives: self-promotion (those things such as newsletters, direct-mail, seminars, events, brochures, etc., which a business does to tell its own story); media relations (the use of media to communicate the message); and advertising (the use of paid space or time to transmit the story).

It is true that a lot of advertising money is wasted, particularly when it is self-serving, thrown together by amateurs, and not targeted at the correct audience. Even big companies make these mistakes. But study after study has shown that advertising contributes to increased sales. And the cumulative effect of a well-planned advertising campaign has been shown to last for up to six months after the campaign has ended.

5. We rely on word-of-mouth for new business. Any strong business relies on word-of-mouth advertising, but an effort should be made to insure that word-of-mouth process is even more effective. One of the goals of the marketing program is to enhance a customer's new reasons for having become customers in the first place. This is accomplished through a a graceful blending of self-promotion, media relations, and advertising. Also, advertising should be directed toward existing customers. The goal in both instances is to keep them coming back—and indicating to them how wise they are to be doing business with your company! All this is what gets the mouths moving!

6. We don't need marketing because everybody knows us. Such a comment is right out of the 1950s. Try telling that to McDonald's, because they'll be glad to save all their marketing money. First, everybody does not think of you when considering a buying decision. If that were the case, only one insurance agency would survive in a community—or one of any other business, for that matter. There's another issue here, too. How many times has someone said to you, "I didn't know you did that?" Probably once a day, if you are honest.

7. Direct mail is nothing but junk mail. Actually, I hope a lot of people continue to think that direct mail is nothing but junk mail. It's great for clients to have so many of their competitors dismissing one of the most cost-effective ways to target both current customers and qualified prospects. I will readily admit that a lot of direct mail falls into the junk category because it is so poorly created and executed. It belongs in the waste basket. But the truth of the matter is that mail does get opened. A recent Louis Harris poll indicated that seventy-six percent of those interviewed eagerly open their mail. Whether it is a newsletter or a sales pitch, direct mail can get tremendous results.

8. Newspapers and business magazines aren't interested in us. Who said so? Certainly they are not going to be interested unless they know who you are, your particular expertise, and what you are doing. There's tremendous power, especially in the print media. Readers are impressed when they see a company's name in print. This makes a strong and lasting impression. Clients tell us how amazed they are at the number of people who comment when an article mentioning them appears in print.

9. Our sales are great, so why waste money on marketing? Many companies are of the opinion that it is good business to carry on a marketing program when sales are strong. We have a number of clients, including ourselves, who do their heaviest marketing during the best times of the year. This is because the marketing process has a cumulative effect—and many times a delayed reaction. Just because you're out there marketing services doesn't mean a particular company is ready for that service. Yet when the need arises, a funny thing happens—they call. That's what marketing is all about.

10. Marketing is only for big companies. Even among very successful businesspeople, there is the mistaken notion that smaller companies cannot really get into marketing. The scale of marketing may be different, but any size company should have a marketing program including specific short- and long-term goals and objectives. Unfortunately, in smaller companies, marketing money is often wasted on irrelevant and absolutely meaningless messages which someone calls advertising, public relations, or marketing. Smaller companies need the best marketing guidance and advice they can get in order to avoid wasting money and to compete effectively. No matter who we are or what business we are in, we're engaged in marketing. It just so happens that some do it better—and smarter—than others.

Marketing is the driving force in today's business world. The better a company is at marketing, the more successful it will be in the marketplace.

Pearls of Wisdom

The trouble with easy customers is that finding them is getting harder and harder.

■

Marketing is simply sales with a college education.

■

You can tell when the economy is picking up—the sales you lose are bigger.

■

There's a basic change in the way we offer our services ... but we've still got to straddle the line between being regarded as a wise advisor or a hawking peddler.

■

Advertising—once we find the answer that works, stay with it. There's not a bunch of equally strong solutions.

■

Clients don't buy services, they buy expectations of a more favorable future ... and you've got to get inside their personal needs and wants.

■

■ Personal Truths of Peter Drucker

1. The business of business is creating customers.

2. Business has only two functions ... marketing and innovation.

■ Index

To order any of
Tom Feltenstein's
Books and tapes

By Visa, Mastercard, or American Express

Call Toll Free
1-800-235-9647
Monday-Friday 8:00 a.m.-6:00 p.m. Eastern Standard Time

—

For a live interpretation of the principles of this book or any
of the following inspirations and formulas for success at your
convention, conference, or sales meeting, call:

TOM FELTENSTEIN'S NEIGHBORHOOD
MARKETING INSTITUTE
44 Cocoanut Row, Suite T-5
Palm Beach, FL 33480
1-800-235-9647
561-655-7822
Fax: 561-832-7502
e-mail: nmi@feltenstein.com

■ Books

Underdog Marketing
Proven Strategies for Out-Marketing the Big Guns
Learn how to think and act like a fierce, invincible underdog. Tom
Feltenstein's highly acclaimed marketing reference book reveals the 35
Principles of Underdog Marketing. *$169*

Encyclopedia of Promotional Tactics
Discover 333 proven new ways to motivate your staff, build repeat business,
and increase your average check with this extraordinary collection of winning promotional tactics. *$169*

**Foodservice Marketing for the '90s: How to Become the #1
Restaurant in Your Neighborhood**
Tom's hot-selling book will show you how to thrive, not merely survive, in
the highly competitive foodservice industry. *$59.95*

■ Seminars

■ **Strategic Planning** — This breakthrough, step-by-step program will
enable you to create a long-range plan with immediate bottom-line impact.

■ **How to Write a Neighborhood Marketing Plan** — You'll learn the
seven key steps to writing a neighborhood marketing plan that will help win
the battle for the hearts, minds, and pocketbooks of your customers.

■ **The Principles of Underdog Marketing** — A power-packed "call to
arms" that will teach you how to win big in the hospitality, foodservice, and
retail industries.

■ **Promotional Tactics that Boost Sales** — Killer promotional tactics that
are cost-effective and simple to implement.

■ Video Tapes

*Underdog Marketing: Proven Strategies for Out-Marketing the Big
Guns.* Tom's electrifying keynote speech at the 7th Annual Foodservice
Marketing War College is a powerful action plan that will arm you with the
strategies and tactics you'll need to become No. 1 in your neighborhood. *$369*

45 Killer Promotional Tactics. The hottest, most creative solutions to your
marketing problems. These low-cost, easy-to-implement tactics will help you
clobber the competition. *$89*